# Unfair Terms in Consumer Agreements

# Unfair Terms in Consumer Agreements

## *The New Rules Explained*

### Nicholas Lockett, LLB

*Barrister, 10 King's Bench Walk, Temple,*
*Tel: 0171 353 2501 (International +44 171 353 2501)*

### Manus Egan, LLB

*Barrister, Thomas More Chambers,*
*Tel: 0171 404 7000 (International +44 171 404 7000)*

John Wiley & Sons
Chichester • New York • Brisbane • Toronto • Singapore

Published in the United Kingdom in 1995 by Chancery Law Publishing Ltd
Baffins Lane, Chichester,
West Sussex PO19 1UD, England

*National*   Chichester 01243 779777
*International*   (+44) 1243 779777

Published in North America by

John Wiley & Sons Inc
7222 Commerce Center Drive
Colorado Springs CO 80919, USA

*British Library Cataloguing in Publication Data*

A copy of the CIP entry for this book is available from the British Library.

ISBN 0471 95274 5

Typeset in 11/13pt Garamond by Mayhew Typesetting, Rhayader, Powys
Printed and bound in Great Britain by Biddles Ltd, Guildford and King's Lynn

This book is printed on acid-free paper responsibly manufactured from sustainable forestation, for which at least two trees are planted for each one used for paper production.

# Contents

# Contents

# *Chapter 1*
# Introduction

## 1. Introduction

The purpose of this work is to examine and analyse critically the     1.1
Union's legislative initiative to protect consumers within the
European Union against unfair terms in consumer contracts. This
introduction to the work serves two purposes. First, it outlines
briefly how the European Union has developed, in order to place
the 1992 programme in context. This is of relevance since the
Unfair Terms in Consumer Contracts Directive is regarded as an
integral part of that programme. Secondly, it explains the
legislative process within the Union and how it affects individual
Member State regulation.

## 2. The Treaty of Rome

The 1992 internal market programme is directly linked to the     1.2
principles of the European Union as set out in its founding
legislative document, the 1957 Treaty of Rome. Those principles
are encapsulated in Article 2 of the Treaty:

> "The Community shall have as its task, by establishing a common
> market and progressively approximating the economic policies of
> Member States, to promote throughout the Community a harmoni-
> ous development of economic activities, a continuous and balanced
> expansion, an increase in stability, an accelerated raising of the
> standard of living and closer relations between the States belonging
> to it."

Although the removal of internal tariff barriers led to the creation
of the customs union by 1968, further progress on economic
harmonisation was piecemeal. It was not until the mid-1980s that
a new impetus towards the completion of the internal market
began. This impetus was primarily derived from the argument that

1

major economic gains would be lost if substantial harmonisation of the Union's relatively fragmented market was not carried out.

## 3. The 1985 White Paper

**1.3**   In 1985 the European Commission published a White Paper on "the completion of the internal market". This document identified 282 legislative proposals, together with a timetable for implementation, for the attainment of the internal market. The White Paper emphasised the liberalisation of service provision on the basis of mutual recognition of Member States' regulation following on from harmonisation of basic principles.

The White Paper was approved by the governments of all the Member States. It was clear, however, that for the measures identified to be implemented within a reasonable timetable, reform of the Union's legislative processes was necessary.

## 4. The Single European Act

**1.4**   To enable implementation of the White Paper's proposals, the Single European Act was introduced and ratified by each Member State in 1987. The Single European Act amended the provisions of the Treaty of Rome. The Act defined the internal market as comprising: "an area without internal frontiers in which the free movement of goods, persons, services and capital is ensured in accordance with the provisions of this Treaty". 31 December 1992 was identified as the date by which the internal market should be established, and from this the catchphrase "1992" arose.

**1.5**   The most important provision in the Single European Act is Article 18 which inserts Article 100A into the Treaty of Rome, amending the Union's decision-making process in relation to the internal market:

> "The Council shall, acting by a qualified majority on a proposal from the Commission in co-operation with the European Parliament and after consulting the Economic and Social Committee, adopt the measures for the approximation of the provisions laid down by law, regulation or administrative action in Member States which have as their object the establishment and functioning of the internal market."

Previously, measures of the type used in completing the internal market were subject to unanimous voting procedures within the Council of Ministers. As a result such measures were all too often defeated through opposition by a single Member State. More than any other provision, this Treaty amendment facilitated the implementation of the White Paper's proposals.

# 5. **European Union institutions**

There are four principal institutions within the European Union (EU): the Council of Ministers; the European Commission; the European Court of Justice; and the European Parliament. The structure and activities of these bodies are briefly examined here in order to assist in understanding how EU measures are enacted. The Economic and Social Committee (ESC) is also examined, since it also plays a role in the passage of Union legislation. **1.6**

## (i) **The Council of Ministers**

The Council consists of representatives of Member State governments, in practice ministers of those national governments. It is the principal governing body of the European Union, responsible, under Article 145 of the Treaty of Rome, for co-ordinating the general economic policies of the Member States and having the power to take decisions. The term "decisions" includes all binding and non-binding Union measures. **1.7**

## (ii) **The Commission**

The Commission is responsible for the administration of the Union – in essence it is the Union's civil service. The Commission, however, also operates on a number of executive and legislative levels, the most important of which, in the context of this work, lies in the initiation of legislation. The Commission's role in the legislative process is examined at section (7) *infra*. **1.8**

The Commission consists of seventeen members appointed by Member State governments for four-year terms. All appointments are renewable. Each Member State has a minimum of one and a maximum of two Commissioners of its nationality. Commissioners are independent of their national governments, undertaking not to seek or accept instructions from any Member State in the discharge of their duties.

### (iii) **The European Court of Justice (ECJ)**

1.9    The European Court of Justice is the judicial body of the European Union, its structure and powers being derived from Articles 164 to 188 of the Treaty of Rome. The Court consists of thirteen judges and six advocates-general, who are appointed by the Member States for six-year terms. The jurisdiction of the Court is provided by Article 177 of the Treaty of Rome, which empowers it to give preliminary rulings concerning:

> "(a) the interpretation of the Treaty;
> (b) the validity and interpretation of acts of the institutions of the Community;
> (c) the interpretation of the statutes of bodies established by an act of the Council, where those statutes so provide."

These rulings are provided in the context of proceedings before national courts or tribunals. Such rulings are at the request of the national courts and are intended to enable them to reach a conclusion on issues of EU law which are before them.

### (iv) **The European Parliament**

1.10   The European Parliament is the only directly elected institution of the Union; it is also, paradoxically, the weakest of the institutions, having no power actually to enact legislation. Of the functions of the European Parliament the only one of relevance in the context of this work is its role in examining draft EU legislation. All legislative proposals are now submitted to the European Parliament for an opinion. It is important to note, however, that the Parliament's opinion in this context is advisory only; it is not binding on either the Council or the Commission.

### (v) **The Economic and Social Committee (ESC)**

1.11   The ESC is composed of 189 members who are appointed for four years by the Council as representatives of various classes of economic and social activity. Although appointed by the Council, the ESC's members may not be bound by mandatory instructions.

The ESC's role is essentially one of consultation and its opinions, as with the European Parliament, do not have to be followed by either the Commission or the Council. In practice, however, the Committee's opinions carry considerable influence in the legislative process and have been effective in bringing about substantial changes in many of the measures adopted by the Union. The Committee's opinions are referred to throughout this work, particularly in relation to legislative measures that are still at the draft stage where the ESC's opinions may be instrumental in bringing about changes before the legislation is finalised.

# 6. **European Union measures**

The European Union has the power to adopt a number of 1.12 different forms of legislative act which vary in their impact on Member States.

## (i) **Regulations**

Regulations are binding and are directly applicable in all Member 1.13 States. Direct applicability means that national measures are not required for a Regulation's provisions to be implemented on a national basis. Furthermore, Member States have no discretion to apply such provisions in a selective manner – Regulations are binding in their entirety. This means that Regulations are the most powerful of the legislative measures available to the Union's institutions.

## (ii) **Directives**

Directives, as with Regulations, can be issued by both the Council 1.14 and the Commission. Directives are also binding on Member States. Directives are not, however, directly applicable, rather they have direct effect. In practice, this means that Member States implement a Directive's provisions through their own national legislative or administrative procedures. A Directive was the legislative form adopted to implement the Union's control of unfair terms in consumer contracts.

### (iii) **Recommendations**

**1.15** Recommendations have no binding force. They are intended to influence Member States in their regulatory approaches. Recommendations, as will be shown, are often used as a precursor to subsequent binding Directives. As with Regulations and Directives, Recommendations can be adopted by both the Council and the Commission.

# 7. **The European Union's legislative process**

**1.16** Given that the legislative measure of primary importance in this work is the Directive, this section will examine the process through which such legislation is enacted.

There are two different methods for the adoption of a Directive, the consultation procedure and the co-operation procedure. Which procedure is followed is dependent upon the Treaty of Rome article upon which a proposed Directive is based.

**1.17** Under the consultation procedure, a Directive is initially proposed by either the Council or the Commission. Next, the Council requests an opinion on the proposed legislation from both the European Parliament and the ESC. Once these opinions have been obtained, the Commission has the opportunity to amend the draft Directive. It should be noted that whilst the Commission has the discretion to follow the opinions of the European Parliament and the ESC, it is not required to do so as such opinions are not binding. Finally, the proposed Directive is placed in front of the Council which has the power to adopt the Directive as proposed, to adopt it in an amended form or, if it fails to reach an agreement, to table it.

**1.18** Initially, the co-operation procedure is the same as the consultation procedure. Opinions are obtained from the European Parliament and the ESC on the draft legislation with the Commission then possessing the opportunity to amend. Thereafter the Council, if in agreement, adopts a common position on the draft legislation. The common position is sent to the European Parliament for a second reading. The Parliament has three months in which to accept, reject or propose amendments to the Directive. The Commission then has a second opportunity to amend the proposal. Finally the draft Directive is returned to the Council which has three months in which to make a final decision. If agreement is not reached within that time period the proposal lapses.

## 8. **Consumer law and the internal market**

The Unfair Terms in Consumer Contracts Directive is arguably the 1.19
most important piece of EU legislation passed in the field of contract law. In Chapter 3 the Directive is examined in detail, from its history and the reasons for its introduction to the test of fairness and provisions for enforcement. Chapter 4 provides an analysis of the indicative Annex of unfair terms and how it should assist in the determination as to what forms of consumer contract terms will no longer be effective.

# Chapter 2

# The Consumer Protection Programmes

## 1. Development

The Unfair Consumer Contract Terms Directive (Dir 93/13/EEC)  **2.1** arose as a result of Resolutions of the European Council, which led to the creation of two preliminary programmes for "consumer protection and information policy". These programmes had the objective of harmonising the legislation within the European Community which was designed to protect the health, safety and economic interests of the consumer as first recognised in the 1972 Paris Summit. The first consumer protection programme of 1974 led to a Council Resolution (OJ 1975 C92/1), which was later expanded into a second consumer protection programme Council Resolution (OJ 1981 C133/1). The stated intention of the programmes was, and remains, to create a level playing field between consumers, sellers and suppliers.

The 1974 programme recognised that there were widespread  **2.2** abuses arising from the growing marketplace, increasing diversity, the complexity of goods and services which are offered to customers and associated services which customers were purchasing with the initial goods and services. The programme argued that in modern society the consumer had gradually failed to maintain a balanced position with the supplier as market conditions changed, and the weight of most contractual terms had, therefore, become heavily slanted in favour of the supplier. Various factors, such as new methods of manufacture, upgrading of technology, new methods of communication and new retailing and financing methods had increased the demand for a variety of goods and services, with the result that the individual consumer had become able to influence only a very small amount of sales volume in a mass national market consisting of large distributors, which contrasted with the former position of a small individual purchaser in a small local market. In addition, the growth of widespread, strongly organised production and distribution groups with the ability to create mass advertising and marketing pressures, and the growth by acquisition, cartel and merger of the supply chain giants, further eroded the ability of consumers to protect their position and adequately to determine market conditions.

# 2. **Member State activity**

**2.3**  It has taken almost 20 years for the type of legislation, identified as being needed, to be adopted and implemented at a Community level. This delay can be explained, in part, by the fact that the 1975 Council Resolution resulted in a flurry of activity on a national level in the field of consumer protection. These early approaches to strengthening consumer protection varied greatly between Member States. In 1976, for example, the Federal Republic of Germany introduced legislation based upon extensive use of grey lists and blacklists of contractual terms which were either voidable or void *ab initio*. The United Kingdom implemented the Unfair Contract Terms Act 1977, which prevented the exclusion of liability for death or personal injury and subjected most other contractual terms to reasonableness tests which often required judicial interpretation. In France, the legislature adopted yet another approach, using administrative law procedures where court judgments were followed by recommendations to government ministers, who then passed the relevant legislation.

**2.4**    The changes in trade practices and the increase in the number of standard contract terms and competition developments acted to accentuate the imbalance between parties and made it more difficult for consumers to remain aware of the rights and remedies available to them.

The European Council recognised that there was a need for comprehensive studies and tests on the quality and usefulness of products and the impact of advertising, price policy, market conditions, selling techniques, general consumer behaviour, and peer and social pressures. It was also recognised that it is only with full information that consumers are empowered to make full use of their resources and to maximise their power to redress the balance between themselves and the supplier.

# 3. **Programmes for reform**

Both programmes drew on the basic EEC premise of "constantly **2.5** improving the living and working conditions of individuals of each Member State" and, under Article 2 of "a continued and balanced expansion, an increase in stability, and an accelerated raising of the standard of living". The Commission, therefore, set out the priority of the measures which were to be achieved and recognised that a speedy harmonisation was undesirable because of the upheaval it would cause to the domestic laws of Member States and the uncertainty which would be created in consumers' minds about their rights. The programme decided upon limited changes in the initial phases on the basis that there would be gradual changes throughout the entire life of the programme.

## (i) **The 1974 programme**

The 1974 programme recognised that the consumer was no longer **2.6** a mere purchaser and user of goods and services for "personal, family or group purposes". It recognised that certain matters affect the consumer, either directly or indirectly, and that these matters needed promotion within the majority of future Community programmes and, in particular, the economic, agricultural, social, environmental, transport and energy programmes and legislation. The five major groups within which it was recognised that direct and indirect pressures could be used to the detriment of the consumer and which therefore needed protection were:

(i)   the right to proper, full and adequate information and education;
(ii)  the right to effective protection against hazards which are likely to affect the health and safety of consumers;
(iii) the right of protection against the damage to consumers' economic interests;
(iv)  the right of redress and provision of facilities for help and advice; and
(v)   the right of the consumer to be consulted and represented in discussions concerning consumers and in the framing of decisions affecting their choices.

A basic principle is that goods and services must not, under **2.7** normal and foreseeable conditions of use, present a risk to the health or safety of the consumer and should be capable of being withdrawn by Member States upon evidence of a risk or likely risk to the consumer and that full warnings of risks associated with the product should be given at the time of contracting.

In particular, the programme sought to protect consumers from physical injury from defective goods and to regulate the substances and preparations which form part of any foodstuffs, creating for foodstuffs an early use of the consumer blacklists now common in EC law. Special rules relating to health and safety and providing for type approval and conformity standards were also considered for machines and electrical equipment.

**2.8**     The Council recognised that certain programmes already existed and identified for special treatment the fields of foodstuffs, cosmetics and detergents, utensils and consumer durables, cars, textiles, toys, dangerous substances, medicines, fertilisers, pesticides and herbicides, veterinary products, animal feedstuffs and materials coming into contact with foodstuffs.

**2.9**     The protection of economic interests reflected that consumers also needed protection against abuse of sellers' powers, especially one-sided contracts, exclusion of essential rights unfairly, harsh credit conditions, demands for payment for unsolicited goods and high-pressure sales methods. The programme also sought to outlaw the misleading presentation and promotion of goods and services (whether directly or indirectly), misleading advertising, misleading information at point of sale, and advertisements. It also sought to provide for reliable after-sales services for consumer durables, proper provision of spare parts and provision of an adequate choice of goods for consumers.

**2.10**    Whilst the measures undertaken by Member States in the 1970s went some way towards the goal, it was still possible, even within the resulting changes, for contracts to be one-sided and for unilateral terms to be imposed.

The Commission, in the first programme, noted an urgent need for protection of consumers' economic interests, especially the harmonisation of consumer credit and hire-purchase facilities, although it did not specify proposals, pending a study by the Commission.

The Commission recognised that there was inadequate advice, help and redress available to consumers. It therefore sought improvements in assistance and advice programmes, redress, arbitration and settlement of disputes and proposals for exchanging information. It also recognised that there should be sufficient information given to the consumer to permit the assessment of the basic features, nature, quality, quantity and price of goods, to make a rational choice between competing products, to use the products safely and to claim redress in the event of failure of the product.

With this in mind, the Commission formulated its intention to produce legislation for clear, understandable and unambiguous labelling schemes and the harmonisation of methods to state prices and the price per unit of volume or weight. It also recommended that there should be a requirement that foodstuffs should state the nature, composition, origin, weight, volume and food-value and include useful date markings.

The first programme did not identify in any great depth the **2.11** steps to be taken for consumer consultation, representation and implementation, but it did list (in Appendix 1) the action which the Community had taken so far to assist the interests of consumers and (in Appendix 2) a selection of Directives of interest to consumers.

## (ii) **The 1981 programme**

In 1981 the Commission adopted its "Programme on Information **2.12** Policy" (OJ 1981 C133) at page 1. This document emphasised the importance of safeguarding consumers with regard to unfair terms which were inserted, usually by sellers and suppliers, into the contract with the consumer.

The second programme for consumer protection and information policy was published in June 1981. It built on the basic building blocks of the first programme and identified that the provisions of the first programme had resulted in the elimination of many of the non-tariff barriers to trade and in the harmonisation of competition rules. The second programme considered that there were two major questions which the Community needed to address in the second programme, namely:

(i)　the price of goods and services, notably within industrial policy, competition policy and the common agricultural policy; and

(ii)　the quality of services.

## 4. **Further attempts at reform**

**2.13**   As a result of their continuing concerns, the Commission published a consultation paper in 1984 entitled "Unfair Terms in Contracts Concluded with Consumers". The paper was circulated widely and resulted in intensive opposition from numerous commercial undertakings in all Member States. These commercial organisations argued unsurprisingly that they should be allowed continued freedom to insert terms of their own choice into standard contracts unilaterally (one term used to describe the proposed legislation was "overprotective"). Consumer organisations, with equal predictability, argued that the ordinary person was in need of greater protection, particularly as the Single Market approached.

**2.14**   During 1985 and 1986 the European Parliament considered the issue of consumer protection within the Legal Affairs Committee and the Public Health, Environmental and Consumer Protection Committee. It accepted the need for increased protection for consumers against the imposition of unfair contract terms. The Legal Affairs Committee went as far as suggesting that the Directive should not be limited to the protection of consumers but should protect all parties whenever there was an imbalance in bargaining strengths (a proposal that was not incorporated into the Directive in its final form).

**2.15**   In mid-1986 the Council adopted a Resolution calling for proposals under the "New Impetus for Consumer Policy", which included the draft Unfair Terms in Consumer Contracts Directive. Urgency was added to the proposals by the Single Market programme, however support for these proposals was not without reservation. The UK's Department of Trade and Industry, for example, doubted that the Single Market, in itself, was sufficient to justify the proposals and expressed misgivings due to the fact that the proposals were substantially broader than existing UK legislation. It concluded, however, that, on balance, it was time for the United Kingdom to move in the direction of the proposed legislation:

> "Unless there is some assurance that they [consumers] will not be seriously disadvantaged by unfair contracts, consumers will lack the confidence to use the new possibilities opened up by the completion of the internal market, for example the opportunity to buy goods and services, at more favourable prices in other Member States than their country of residence."

## 5. **Directive on Unfair Terms in Consumer Contracts**

The Directive on Unfair Terms in Consumer Contracts (DIR 93/13/ **2.16** EEC) was adopted as a common position on 22 September 1992 and made final on 21 April 1993. It was subject to qualified majority voting by Member States under Article 100A of the EC Treaty, as well as being subject to approval by the Council of Ministers, the European Parliament and the Commission under the co-operation procedure (*see* para 1.5). The Directive became law on 1 January 1995 and will apply to all contracts concluded after that date.

The Council identified that the consumer policy had been **2.17** defensive in the first programme and that the second programme should have a more positive role, establishing the consumer as a party involved in the preparation and implementation of consumer-based economic decisions, and that the consumers' views should always be taken into account whenever policy was formulated. To achieve this it was recognised that a universal test of fairness was needed and that a disincentive should be created to prevent the spread of terms that were not negotiated but came from standard terms and which operated as oppressive and unfair to the consumer.

The Council also noted that education of consumers was of **2.18** paramount importance and that facilities should be available to both young and old, to educate them into discriminating consumers able to make fully informed choices and being conscious of their rights and responsibilities. The Commission also stated that as a priority measure Member States should consider introducing consumer education into schools and create programmes of consumer training.

The Commission also envisaged the creation of voluntary **2.19** programmes and formulae which should act in parallel with the existing legislation and regulation available at Community level. The programme envisaged that the Commission would look at creating more informed consumer choice by a voluntary comparison-testing scheme.

The Council identified areas of animal nutrition, food, human **2.20** and veterinary pharmaceuticals, pesticides, cosmetics, textile and flammability, toy safety, toxicology and ecotoxicology as areas of remaining concern and stated that it would look to a complete harmonisation of laws on labelling, presentation and advertising of foodstuffs and uses of flavouring, surface sprays on fruits, vegetables and cheeses, baby foods, deep-frozen foods and pesticide residues. The Council sought to introduce an early warning system for unexpected health problems and a system for information concerning accidents involving consumer products.

In the field of protection of the economic interests of consumers, the Council proposed Directives on contracts negotiated away from business premises, misleading and unfair advertising, defective product liability, consumer services and consumer credit. The Commission also identified that there was a need to legislate for the abuses within the fields of after-sales services for consumer durables and especially with a view to forcing an increase in the length of useful life of household durables.

**2.21** The Commission identified that anti-competitive behaviour was possible by manufacturers who failed to use the latest scientific knowledge and production techniques and materials in order to extend the life of their products to the longest reasonably possible. The Commission, in so identifying gave clear guidance to manufacturers of high-cost consumer durables that if the life of products was not extended by the manufacturers voluntarily then the Commission would respond by various provisions in a future Directive.

**2.22** The Commission also identified that the quality of after-sales service varied widely and that maintenance and repairs were a source of concern, together with the provisions and terms and conditions of guarantees. The Commission gave notice that it would be looking at a requirement to draw up detailed estimates and invoices; consumers would be entitled to an explanation if these estimates were exceeded or if there was any excess in transport costs, out-of-service costs or the costs of replacement parts. Under the new Directive, challenges to any additional costs in excess of the estimates given will now be possible on the grounds that they are a unilateral change in the agreed terms and are a breach of the Annex guidelines.

**2.23** The Commission identified anti-competitive practices concerning warranties and sales terms which operated against the consumer by the use of unfair contract terms and gave notice that priority would be given to the improvement of the position of the consumer with regard to contract terms, warranties and services associated with consumer durables, vehicles and electrical household goods. Many of the terms used in guarantees and warranties to limit the liability of the supplier will now fail under the general good faith test or if they are an unfair standard term or outlawed by the Annex.

The Commission, whilst not proposing immediately to imple- **2.24** ment a Directive aimed at public utilities within the second programme, gave a clear intention that it would, in the near future, be considering a public and quasi-public utility Directive in the fields of electricity, gas, water supplies and transport, to properly protect the consumer against public bodies, privatised monopolies and similar bodies providing a public service. It also identified concern with the proper protection of underprivileged consumers and that particular steps would have to be taken to properly protect the particular needs of these consumers. It is to be expected, therefore, that a Directive on consumer contracts for public and quasi-public service will be produced in due course.

The Commission sought to look at the position of legal aid and **2.25** legal standing in the Community and, as priority measures, to study the channels and procedures for obtaining legal remedies. In particular, the right of consumer associations to institute legal proceedings, the simplification of court procedures, the processing of individual petitions and the creation of a proper alternative dispute-resolution procedure were examined. The Commission sought to identify the admissibility of proceedings by consumers against public undertakings and quasi-undertakings administered on a commercial basis. The Directive clearly envisages that Consumer Protection Associations will have the necessary standing to mount challenges to unfair terms, although it fails to expressly create the standing where this is deficient in national law, and the standing must therefore be implied into domestic law via the Directive.

Finally the Commission also looked at the need to properly **2.26** inform and educate consumers and considered that it was desirable that consumers should be able properly to assess the value for money of products and services (particularly as regards warranties and after-sales service). The Commission determined that more information should be detailed on products and provision would have to be made for customers to be able to compare identical products where the products were not readily identifiable as substantially the same. The Commission also envisaged that these measures would entail some change to regulations on price marking.

# 6. **Conclusion**

**2.27** Whilst the programme has been largely implemented in principle, there have remained a number of glaring loopholes through which the manufacturers and providers of services have been able to avoid their obligations to consumers and through which the proper protection of the consumer has not been achieved. The Unfair Consumer Contract Terms Directive has gone some way to closing many of the loopholes although even after the implementation of this Directive there will still be a number of areas of the programme which are not fully in place; in particular there will be large numbers of people in the Member States, classified by the Commission as the underprivileged consumer who will remain largely ignorant of their rights or who, by nature of their circumstances, are vulnerable to abuse of their position as consumer.

**2.28**      This Directive falls short of protecting this group adequately, particularly with the ambiguity which exists (and which is discussed later in this book) concerning the ability of the consumer associations to commence pre-emptive actions against terms and conditions which they deem unfair.

# Chapter 3

# The Unfair Terms in Consumer Contracts Directive

## 1. Introduction

On 5 April 1993 the European Union adopted Directive 93/13/EEC **3.1** on Unfair Terms in Consumer Contracts (OJ 1993 L95/29). The purpose of this legislation is to protect consumers within the European Union against unfair contractual terms. The Directive is viewed as a necessary element in the creation of the internal market through the "1992" programme. Under that programme, Member States' internal frontiers relating to goods, persons, services and capital have been removed with the purpose of stimulating and increasing trade between these countries. Currently, there are many disparities between Member State laws in relation to the regulation of contractual terms between sellers of goods or suppliers of services and the consumers of such goods and services. Such disparities can distort competition amongst such sellers and suppliers when they attempt to carry on their trade in other Member States. Moreover, most consumers are ignorant of the laws governing consumer contracts in countries other than their own. As a result, consumers may be deterred from becoming involved in transactions based in Member States other than their own. This is likely to be particularly the case where the contract is drafted in a language foreign to the consumer. Thus the Directive is viewed as a measure that facilitates the creation of the internal market; provides an important element of consumer protection on an EU-wide basis; stimulates inter-Member State consumer transactions by increasing consumer confidence; assists sellers and suppliers in their task of selling goods and supplying services throughout the European Union; and increases competition, thereby increasing choice for the European Union's consumers.

## 2. **Parties to the contract**

**3.2**    Article 2 defines a "seller or supplier" as anyone, whether a natural or legal person, who, in the context of being a party to a contract covered by the provisions of the Directive, acts for trade, business or professional purposes. This definition applies whether the seller or supplier acts for or on behalf of a public or privately owned commercial entity.

A "consumer" is any natural person who, with regard to contracts covered by the Directive, acts for purposes outside trade, business or profession.

**3.3**    In its Opinion (OJ 1991 C159) at page 34, the Economic and Social Committee (ESC) recommended that the Commission consider, in the very near future, the possibility of prohibiting unfair terms in all contracts, whether or not a consumer is a party. The purpose of such an approach would be to provide similar protection to small and medium-sized enterprises, otherwise known as SMEs. As can be seen from the definition of consumer, however, such an approach was not incorporated into the Directive in its final form. However, future EU legislation in this field cannot be ruled out.

## 3. **Exempted contracts**

**3.4**    The preamble states that, for the purposes of effective consumer protection, the Directive's rules on unfair terms should apply to all contracts concluded between sellers or suppliers and consumers. Paradoxically, the preamble then proceeds to exclude certain contracts from the provisions of the Directive. Contracts in the following areas are excluded:

- employment
- succession rights
- rights under family law
- incorporation and organisation of companies
- partnership agreements

**3.5**    Terms in insurance contracts which define and circumscribe the insured risk and the insurer's liability are not subject to the test of fairness. The preamble states that this is because such restrictions are taken into account when the premium paid by the consumer is calculated. This partial exclusion of insurance contracts from the provisions of the Directive derives from the fact that terms describing the subject-matter of the contract and/or the quality/ price ratio of the goods or services supplied are not subject to the test of unfairness. This exclusion is examined at para 3.14.

Article 1(2) declares that contractual terms which reflect **3.6** mandatory statutory or regulatory provisions are not to be made subject to the provisions of the Directive. This exclusion also extends to provisions or principles of international conventions to which the Member States of the Community are party. This exclusion applies particularly to the area of transport. It is interesting to note that, in terms of specific contractual areas excluded, this is the only one that is specified in both the preamble and the main body of the Directive. The preamble identifies the reason behind this exclusion as being the presumption that such consumer contracts do not contain unfair terms.

Finally, the preamble states that the Directive will apply only to contracts which have *not* been individually negotiated with the consumer, regardless of whether the contract has been concluded by word of mouth or in writing. This issue is examined in more detail at para 3.7 *infra*.

# 4. The test of fairness

## (i) The distinction between negotiated and non-negotiated contracts

The test of fairness is set out in Articles 3 and 4 of the Directive. **3.7** The first stage in deciding whether a contractual term is fair or unfair is to determine whether it has been individually negotiated. Only contractual terms which have not been individually negotiated are covered by the Directive. One reason for this approach is that the Directive only seeks to achieve partial harmonisation. The Directive draws such a distinction between negotiated and non-negotiated contracts because in the latter case the consumer is unable to influence the substance of the term.

In many situations, it will be a relatively easy matter to conclude **3.8** whether a contract has been individually negotiated or not. To assist, the Directive defines a term as not being individually negotiated where it has been drafted in advance and, in particular, where it is part of a pre-formulated standard contract. Problems may arise, however, where a contract contains both terms which have been individually negotiated and terms which have not. The Directive makes specific provision for such cases. It states that where part of a term or an entire term has been individually negotiated the application of the Directive to the rest of the contract shall not be excluded, if, on an overall assessment of the contract, it appears that it is a pre-formulated standard contract. Even with these provisions, difficulties remain in interpreting the Directive where the seller or supplier offers alternative terms from a pool of standard terms. It may be argued that the individual terms are caught by the Directive as they are pre-drafted, but the contrary view may be that the terms, although pre-drafted, have also been individually negotiated by the consumer and therefore the consumer has been able to influence the substance of the term by determining whether it was to be included or not.

**3.9**     The burden of proof lies upon any seller or supplier who wishes to argue that a standard term has been individually negotiated. This is a reversal of the general legal obligation in most Member States where the party making an assertion is required to discharge the burden of proof. In cases resulting from this Directive, it will normally be the consumer or consumer association who asserts that the term or terms in issue have not been individually negotiated. It will then fall to the seller or supplier, on the balance of probabilities, to disprove that assertion.

## (ii) **Factors determining fairness/unfairness**

**3.10**  Once it has been determined that a contractual term in a consumer contract has not been individually negotiated, the next stage is to determine whether, contrary to the requirement of good faith, it causes a significant imbalance in the parties' rights and obligations arising under the contract, where that imbalance acts to the detriment of the consumer. It should be stated that the term "good faith" does not, in the context of this Directive, have the meaning attached to it by law in many Member States. In the United Kingdom, for example, a thing is deemed to be done in good faith when it is in fact done honestly, whether it is done negligently or not (Sale of Goods Act 1979, s 61(3); Bills of Exchange Act 1882, s 90). The preamble, for the purposes of this Directive, provides a completely different definition when it states:

"Whereas the assessment, according to the general criteria chosen, of the unfair character of terms, in particular in sale or supply activities of a public nature providing collective services which take account of solidarity among users, must be supplemented by a means of making an overall evaluation of the different interests involved; *whereas this constitutes the requirement of good faith*; whereas, in making an assessment of good faith, particular regard shall be had to the strength of the bargaining positions of the parties, whether the consumer had an inducement to agree to the term and whether the goods or services were sold or supplied to the special order of the consumer; *whereas the requirement of good faith may be satisfied by the seller or supplier where he deals fairly and equitably with the other party whose legitimate interests he has taken into account;*" (italics added)

It appears, therefore, that any attempt to rely on national defi- **3.11** nitions of good faith, thereby limiting the definition of unfairness, in the case of the United Kingdom, to whether the seller or supplier had acted honestly, would fail in the light of the above definition of the term. This point is supported by the fact that several of the potentially unfair terms indicated in the Annex could not be affected by the question as to whether the seller or supplier acted honestly or dishonestly. It should be noted that the matters identified above are not meant to be an exhaustive list of considerations in determining whether the requirement of good faith has been satisfied and that other factors may be considered where appropriate.

In applying the test of unfairness, the most crucial consideration **3.12** is whether the contractual term in issue causes a significant imbalance in the parties' rights and obligations. All of the factors listed above are relevant to that determination. The term "significant imbalance", however, although not defined in the Directive, would indicate that cases involving minor detriment to the consumer will not be construed as unfair.

Article 4 provides that in determining whether a contractual **3.13** term is fair or unfair consideration must be given to the nature of the goods and services to which the contract relates and, at the time the contract is concluded, all the other terms of the contract. In other words, an overall assessment of the contract needs to be made. Examples of the factors to be taken into consideration are identified in the above quotation. Thus, for example, a term that might otherwise be determined to be unfair may be saved by the fact that the consumer accepted a material inducement to agree to the term's inclusion. A major consideration, also listed above, will be the strength of the bargaining positions of the respective parties. This factor overlaps with the issue of whether the contract is negotiable or non-negotiable, as a consumer's bargaining position in respect of a non-negotiated contract is very limited indeed. The Directive identifies a further important criteria, in that if the contract in question is dependent upon any other contract, that other contract must be taken into consideration.

Finally, the Directive provides useful guidance as to terms which may be considered unfair in the indicative Annex of unfair terms. The Annex is examined in far greater detail in Chapter 4.

### (iii) The position of subject matter and price/ratio terms

**3.14**  The relevance of the subject matter of the contract in assessing unfairness is somewhat ambiguous. As stated above, it is a consideration when determining the validity of a particular term. However, the Directive goes on to state:

> "Assessment of the unfair nature of the terms shall relate neither to the definition of the main subject matter of the contract nor to the adequacy of the price and remuneration, on the one hand, as against the services or goods supplied in exchange, on the other, in so far as these terms are in plain intelligible language."

**3.15**  At first glance, these two approaches appear to contradict one another. Fortunately, the preamble provides an explanation. It states that in assessing the fairness or unfairness of a contractual term the nature of the goods or services should have an influence. However, terms which directly describe the main subject matter of the contract or the price/ratio quality shall not be subject to the test of fairness. In other words, whilst such terms are relevant in making an overall assessment of the fairness of terms which are subject to this Directive, they cannot be assessed solely in their own right. This exclusion from the Directive's provisions is itself limited by the qualification that such terms should be in plain and intelligible language. Thus subject matter and price/ratio terms which fail the requirement of intelligibility will succumb to the test of fairness. The approach taken to such terms is logical given the method by which the Directive deals with contractual terms which are deemed unfair (*see* para 3.19).

A general difficulty in dealing with "main subject matter" terms **3.16** lies in actually identifying which terms of the contract fall within this category. "Main subject matter" is not defined in the Directive; as a result Member States may vary in their approach, with certain countries applying the partial exclusion afforded in this area to terms that other countries do not exclude. This difficulty, however, may be reduced by the Directive's requirement that such terms be in plain intelligible language.

## 5. The requirement of intelligibility

The Directive provides that where all or some of the terms of the **3.17** contract are in writing, such terms must always be drafted in plain, intelligible language (Art 5). The Directive adds an incentive for sellers and suppliers to draft such contracts plainly and intelligibly by providing that where there is any doubt about the meaning of a term, the interpretation most favourable to the consumer shall prevail. The preamble identifies a further addendum on this point when it states that consumers should be given the opportunity to examine all the terms of the contract. The use of the word "examine" is ambiguous. It is unclear, for example, whether sellers and suppliers will merely have to provide the consumer with the contractual document or whether they must ensure that the consumer understands the effect of the relevant contractual terms. The ESC suggested several amendments in this area. The consumer, for example, should be entitled to make himself acquainted with the terms of the contract (*e.g.* through physical delivery of the contract, shop posters and the like). Another recommendation was to place an obligation upon the seller or supplier to inform the consumer of the terms applicable to the contract. A third option that was mooted was to make transparency of a contractual term an additional criterion of fairness. None of these proposals was directly incorporated into the Directive. It is submitted that this lack of clarification is unfortunate as it provides further scope for variations in approach between different Member States and will, no doubt, be an issue involving substantial judicial consideration throughout the European Union.

It must be noted that the requirement of intelligibility applies **3.18** not only to contractual terms which normally fall within the ambit of the Directive but also to terms describing the subject matter of the contract as well as the price/ratio quality (*see* para 3.14). If it can be argued that such terms have not been drafted in a plain and intelligible fashion then the test of fairness is applicable. It should be noted, however, that where a consumer or consumer organisation relies upon the provisions in Article 7 to seek judicial or administrative determination as to whether certain contractual terms are fair or unfair, the requirement of intelligibility is not necessarily applicable.

# 6. **The effect of unfair terms**

**3.19**  The Directive requires Member States to provide, under national law, that terms in consumer contracts that are determined to be unfair shall not be binding on the consumer. If such a step is taken, however, it does not necessarily mean that the contract comes to an end. Contracts will continue to be effective and will bind all parties upon the terms which are not deemed to be unfair if the contract is capable of continuing in existence without the unfair terms.

**3.20**      The fact that consumer contracts may continue to be effective even if they contain non-binding unfair terms explains the approach taken by the Directive to terms relating to subject matter and/or price quality ratio. Such terms are fundamental to the contract. Were they to be deemed non-binding it would, in virtually all cases, be impossible for the contract to continue. It is therefore sensible not to submit such terms, save for the requirement of intelligibility, to the test of unfairness.

# 7. **Contracts concluded in a non-Member State**

**3.21**  Problems with regard to the application of this Directive may arise where a consumer residing in a Member State enters into a contract which purports to be governed by the law of a country which is not part of the European Union. Potentially, sellers and suppliers desiring to rely upon terms in consumer contracts which would otherwise be deemed to be unfair could circumvent the

# Unfair Terms Directive

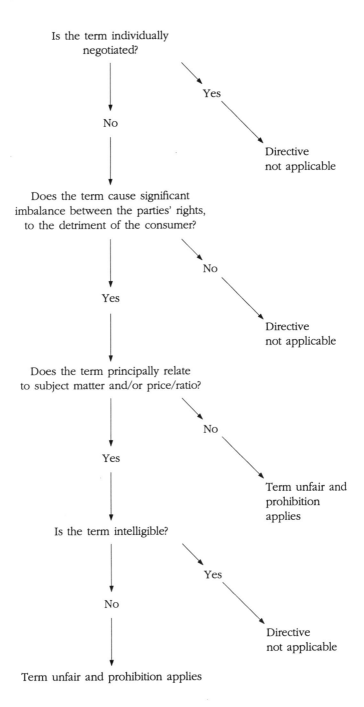

Is the term individually negotiated?

No

Yes → Directive not applicable

Does the term cause significant imbalance between the parties' rights, to the detriment of the consumer?

Yes

No → Directive not applicable

Does the term principally relate to subject matter and/or price/ratio?

Yes

No → Term unfair and prohibition applies

Is the term intelligible?

No

Yes → Directive not applicable

Term unfair and prohibition applies

Directive by including provisions placing such contracts under the jurisdiction of a non-EU country. The Directive recognises this potential lacuna and takes measures to proscribe it (Art 6(2)). Thus Member States are required to take the necessary measures to avert this risk and to ensure that the consumer does not lose the protection provided by the Directive. The proscription applies even if the non-EU country in question has a close connection with the territory of a Member State.

# 8. The requirement to prevent unfair terms in consumer contracts

**3.22**  Potentially, the most important provisions in the Directive are contained in Article 7 which place obligations upon Member States to prevent the continued use of unfair terms in consumer contracts.

The article begins with a general requirement that "adequate and effective means exist" to prevent such continued use. This general requirement is viewed as being in the interests of both consumers and competitors of sellers and suppliers who seek to rely upon unfair terms.

**3.23**  The general requirement does not stand alone. Article 7 goes on to stipulate that Member States must make provision for persons or organisations having a legitimate interest under national law in protecting consumers to enable them to bring an action, under national law, before either their courts or competent adminis-trative bodies. The purpose of such action will be to determine whether contractual terms drawn up for general use are unfair. Should such judicial bodies decide that the term or terms in question are unfair, they will be empowered to apply "appropriate and effective means to prevent the continued use of such terms". The European Parliament (OJ 1991 C326/108) emphasised the particular need for authorised consumer protection offices and organisations to be entitled to take such action.

**3.24**  Individuals or consumer organisations bringing such an action may do so either separately against an individual seller or supplier or jointly against a number of sellers and suppliers from the same economic sector who use the same or similar general contractual terms. The Directive also permits actions against the trade associations of such sellers and suppliers which recommend the use of the contractual terms in question. The preamble states that the right to bring such actions is not intended to allow for prior verification of the general conditions obtaining in individual economic sectors. Thus sellers, suppliers and their associations will not be entitled to pre-empt any determination of terms by the courts through bringing their own actions to decide the validity of contractual clauses that they wish to continue to rely upon.

A fundamental factor influencing the effectiveness of these **3.25** provisions will be the process by which the relevant courts or administrative bodies determine whether a person or organisation wishing to bring an action has the requisite standing or *locus standi*. The preamble states that such applicants must have a "legitimate interest in the matter"; the Directive states that they must have "a legitimate interest under national law in protecting consumers". The latter provision is, of course, the more authoritative.

By conferring access to the relevant courts or administrative **3.26** bodies upon organisations which have a legitimate interest in protecting consumers, the Directive has greatly increased the possibilities for the effective enforcement of its provisions. Enforcement by individuals of consumer law provisions is, for obvious reasons, often ineffective. Financial and procedural considerations will normally be sufficient to deter a consumer from pursuing litigation. By conferring the right to litigate upon consumer associations the problems of private enforcement are sidestepped. One can therefore view the provisions of Article 7 as a method by which the Directive removes the "significant imbalance" between consumer and seller/supplier from the litigation process for the regulation of unfair terms.

By leaving the determination of fairness to the discretion of **3.27** individual Member States' judicial systems there is an obvious danger that different approaches to the same types of contractual terms will develop. Both the ESC and the European Parliament recognised this problem and made several recommendations to minimise it. The ESC proposed that decisions by judicial or administrative bodies concerning the implementation of the Directive be notified to the Commission. This would have enabled the Commission to easily monitor developments in different Member States and identify diversity of interpretation. This proposal was not incorporated into the Directive in its final form. The ESC also recommended that the European Court of Justice (ECJ) should be given a major role in determining the judicial approach to the test of fairness. The Directive, however, contains no specific provisions to that effect. The ECJ's role, therefore, will be limited to its normal function of passing judgment on cases referred by national courts.

**3.28**    A key recommendation by the European Parliament relating to the effective prevention of unfair terms in consumer contracts was that an ombudsman's institution should be set up in the Union. The Parliament recommended that an individual article of the Directive should be devoted to this point and suggested the following wording:

> "1.   A Community Ombudsman shall be appointed with the task of:
> (a)   monitoring the application of this Directive by the Member States and requesting the Commission, where necessary, to initiate the procedure laid down in Article 169 of the EEC Treaty against a Member State failing to fulfil its obligations;
> (b)   endeavouring to settle by amicable agreement disputes relating to unfair terms, bringing together parties having their permanent residence in two or more Member States;
> (c)   drawing up an annual report on unfair terms, giving an account of his activities and proposing any reform he considers appropriate, particularly amendments or additions to the compulsory list of unfair terms annexed to this Directive. This report shall be forwarded to the Commission, the Member States and the European Parliament.
> 2.   In exercising his duties, the Ombudsman may require notification of any information he considers necessary for his work. National and Community administrations shall give him all the assistance he needs.
> 3.   The Ombudsman shall be appointed for five years by the Commission, subject to the assent of the European Parliament adopted by a majority of its Members. His term of office shall not be renewable.
> 4.   The Ombudsman shall be assisted by an Ombudsman's Office, composed of officials and other servants appointed by the Ombudsman and subject to the Staff Regulations applicable to officials and conditions of employment of other servants of the European Communities."

**3.29**  As with the ESC's recommendations designed to minimise diversity of approach, the recommendation for an ombudsman has not been adopted. It is submitted that the failure to implement any of the above recommendations is unfortunate as it means that no direct mechanism will exist to ensure a compatible Union-wide approach to the interpretation of terms in consumer contracts.

# 9. **Minimum requirements**

Article 8 provides the following: "Member States *may* [italics 3.30 added] adopt or retain the most stringent provisions compatible with the Treaty in the area covered by this Directive, to ensure a maximum degree of protection for the consumer." The preamble supplements this provision by stating that Member States have the right to continue or, indeed, introduce national legislation which afford consumers a higher level of protection than that stipulated in the Directive. In other words, the Directive's provisions are minimum requirements. The use of minimum requirements is common to many EU legislative initiatives. The most obvious point to be made with regard to their use is that they can easily lead to variation in the impact of the Directive in different Member States. This possibility is increased by the fact that the detailed list of potentially unfair terms, contained in the Annex, is of indicative value only. The potential for variation may prove detrimental to the creation of the internal market as it could create a competitive imbalance between sellers and suppliers situated in different Member States. Take a purely theoretical example: Member State A possesses legislation giving effect to clause (a) of the Annex, identifying any contractual term purporting to exclude or limit liability in the event that an act or omission by a seller or supplier results in the death or personal injury of a consumer, as unfair and prohibiting its effectiveness. Member State B possesses no such legislation and allows such terms to remain effective. The result is that sellers or suppliers situated in Member State B will have a competitive advantage over those based in Member State A since their potential liabilities and insurance requirements will be less and their profitability therefore greater. Following this line of reasoning, it is submitted that the relevance of Article 8 is, itself, minimal. On the basis of purely commercial considerations, Member State regulatory bodies would be advised to comply with the provisions of the Directive and not provide consumer protection in excess of that provided in other Member States.

# 10. **Implementation and review**

Member States are required to bring into force the provisions 3.31 contained in the Directive no later than 31 December 1994 (Art

10). In any event, the Directive will be applicable to all contracts concluded after that date. Indirectly, this implies that it is not intended for the Directive to have retrospective effect. This is entirely understandable, should the Directive have such an effect it would result in an avalanche of litigation, undermining the interests of most commercial undertakings situated within the Community. The term "concluded" indicates that the Directive applies to contracts entered into and binding after 31 December 1994. Thus, where contractual negotiations begin prior to the implementation date but the contract only becomes binding after that date, the Directive's provisions will have effect.

**3.32**    The Commission is required to present a report concerning the application of the Directive to the European Parliament and Council no later than 31 December 1999. Amendments to the Directive, based upon its effect over that five-year period, may follow.

# 11. **Conclusion**

**3.33**  The Unfair Terms in Consumer Contracts Directive is, without doubt, a fundamentally important piece of consumer protection legislation. For the first time ot will introduce the concept of fairness into the law of contract in most Member States. Many of its requirements will increase the quality of consumer protection in most of the Member States: placing the burden of proof upon sellers and suppliers as to whether a particular term has been individually negotiated and, when the issue is one of intelligibility, ensuring that the interpretation most favourable to the consumer shall prevail, are just two, albeit important, examples. The Directive, however, sets out to attain only partial, not full, harmonisation. Examples of this limited approach are the fact that the Directive applies only to non-negotiated contracts and the fact that the list of terms contained in the Annex is of indicative value only and is non-exhaustive. As a result, divergent approaches to consumer contracts may continue to exist in different Member States with certain terms deemed fair in some countries and unfair in others. Thus the objectives behind this legislation, facilitating the internal market and increasing consumer confidence, have only been partly achieved. Whether the Directive is the final step taken by the Community in this important area or merely an intermediate advance towards full harmonisation remains to be seen.

*Chapter 4*

# Indicative List of Contractual Terms

## 1. Introduction

In its draft form, the Directive contained a black list of contractual **4.1** terms, both general and specific, which were to be forbidden. There was considerable opposition amongst several Member States to such a hardline approach, not least because it would require extensive changes in the legislative provisions of those countries. As a result of these concerns, the proposals in respect of the contractual terms contained in the Annex were diluted. Article 3.3 of the Directive in its final form refers to the terms contained in the list as an *indicative* and non-exhaustive list which *may* be regarded as unfair. The preamble is more expansive, it states that: *"for the purposes of this Directive, the annexed list of terms can be of indicative value only and, because of the cause of the minimal character of the Directive, the scope of these terms may be the subject of amplification or more restrictive editing by the Member States in their national laws."*

It is therefore clear that the terms contained in the Annex need **4.2** not necessarily be deemed unfair in a Member State and are only an indication as to unfairness. Member States retain the discretion, in national legislation used to implement the Directive, to permit terms that fall within the Annex to be construed as fair. Such terms, however, will remain vulnerable to the test of fairness, as analysed in Chapter 3, and it will be difficult for a seller or supplier to rely upon such terms given the general guidance that the Annex provides. Member States also retain the discretion to prohibit terms of a category or categories that do not fall within the Annex. This is because of "the minimal character of the Directive". This concept, otherwise known as "minimum requirements", is examined in more detail in Chapter 3.

The Annex can be regarded as a valuable guide for consumers, **4.3** sellers and suppliers as well as legal practitioners as to the types of contractual terms that are likely to be deemed unfair. A brief glance at the list indicates that many types of terms commonly and legitimately used in many Member States will be vulnerable. Thus terms attempting to exclude or limit liability for negligence; permitting retention of deposits; legitimising unseen terms; allowing for exclusive interpretation rights; and tolerating unilateral dissolution or changes to contract and prices by sellers or suppliers are likely to be construed as invalid.

The remainder of this chapter is devoted to examining each type of contractual term listed in the Annex in detail.

## 2. Death and/or injury exclusion clauses

**4.4**   (a)   *excluding or limiting the legal liability of a seller or supplier in the event of the death of a consumer or personal injury to the latter resulting from an act or omission of that seller or supplier*

Most Member States already possess some form of legislation prohibiting terms which attempt to exclude or limit liability in the event of the consumer suffering death or injury. In the United Kingdom, for example, section 2 of the Unfair Contract Terms Act 1977 invalidates any term excluding or restricting liability for death or personal injury resulting from negligence. The Directive, however, refers to terms excluding or limiting liability resulting from an act or omission of the seller or supplier, not merely a negligent act or omission, and in this respect it would appear that the Directive places the equivalent of a higher standard of care upon the seller or supplier than the test of negligence. Thus the effect of this term of the Annex may be to increase protection for the consumer even in those Member States which already regulate such terms. The European Parliament recommended that personal injury specifically include suffering or impairment of health but this wider term, however, was not implemented.

## 3. Legal rights limitation clauses

**4.5**   (b)   *inappropriately excluding or limiting the legal rights of the consumer vis-à-vis the seller or supplier or another party in the event of total or partial non-performance or inadequate* *performance by the seller or supplier of any of the contractual obligations, including the option of offsetting a debt owed to the seller or supplier against any claim which the consumer may have against him*

In its response to the draft Directive, the European Parliament recommended the inclusion of several types of terms which aimed to limit or exclude the seller or supplier's liability in the event of inadequate performance of the contractual obligations by the latter party. In its final form, the Directive incorporated paragraph (b) as a "catch-all" provision, designed to ensure that the seller or supplier could not inappropriately rely upon such clauses by excluding or limiting the consumer's legal rights should they fail to satisfy their contractual obligations. As with a number of the indicative provisions contained in the Annex, the Directive does not seek a blanket prohibition of such terms, rather it suggests that such terms should be deemed unfair where they are "inappropriate". "Inappropriate" is not defined in the Directive and it may therefore give rise to litigation as parties seek to determine what is and is not included within the definition. Moreover, different Member States may continue to vary in their approach to the regulation of this type of term, thereby undermining the harmonising objectives of the Directive. Similar criticism can be made of other sections of the Annex where the undefined term "inappropriate" is used.

**4.6** Paragraph (b) provides one example of what would amount to an inappropriate limitation of the consumer's legal rights by stating that the seller or supplier should not be able to contract out of the consumer's right to set off debts owed by the seller or supplier against any claim that the consumer may have against that party. In most Member States the right of set-off exists. It is often the case, however, that contracting parties retain the right to contract out of this right. This Annex provision will make it difficult, if not impossible, for sellers or suppliers to continue to limit the rights of consumers in such a fashion.

**4.7** Paragraph (b) overlaps with paragraph (q) (*see* para 4.40) which seeks to proscribe contractual terms limiting or excluding the consumer from taking legal action. The latter provision, however, concentrates to a greater degree on claims relating to procedural and evidential matters. The European Parliament sought to add a term covering the seller's breach in the event of *force majeure*; however, this did not appear in the final form of the Directive. It is envisaged that the majority of sellers and suppliers will be able to continue to rely on a *force majeure* clause albeit that there are no express provisions in the Directive. Any such clause would fall to be determined under the test of "inappropriately excluding or limiting" and in many cases it is likely to be judged appropriate to include a *force majeure* clause within a consumer contract.

# 4. Conditional service provisions

**4.8** (c) *making an agreement binding on the consumer whereas provision of services by the seller or supplier is subject to a condition whose realisation depends on his own will alone*

This provision is particularly relevant to the lending industry and to bodies involved in hire-purchase, leasing and similar contractual arrangements. This is because terms binding the consumer to such contracts before irrevocably binding the supplier are in common use. Paragraph (c) will effectively mean that, at best, sellers or suppliers will have to bind themselves to consumer contracts at the same time as the contracting consumer. In practice, sellers and suppliers are likely to protect their positions through increased use of "cooling off periods" which will ensure that sellers or suppliers become bound to the contract before the consumer becomes finally bound.

# 5. Retention of deposit clauses

**4.9** (d) *permitting the seller or supplier to retain sums paid by the consumer where the latter decides not to conclude or perform the contract, without providing for the consumer to receive compensation of an equivalent amount from the seller or supplier where the latter is the party cancelling the contract*

The Directive does not seek to prohibit retention or part-payment clauses in the event of the consumer failing to conclude or perform the contract. Instead it aims to ensure that the consumer receives equal protection through being entitled to compensation of an equivalent amount in the event of the seller or supplier cancelling the contract. Thus sellers and suppliers seeking to rely upon such retention clauses will have to include terms which provide for equal compensation in the event of default of supply. The absence of such a compensation term will make it impossible for the seller or supplier to retain the deposit or arrangement fee if the consumer cancels the contract before the contract is performed.

The European Parliament recommended that the level of **4.10** compensation to be paid to the consumer in such circumstances be double the amount that has been paid or deposited with the seller or supplier at the time of cancellation. This proposal would have further deterred sellers or suppliers from unreasonably terminating contracts or seeking to include retention of deposit terms but regretably, the clause was not included.

The provisions of paragraph (d) considerably overlap with those contained in paragraph (e), which seeks to preclude disproportionately high compensation clauses (*see* para 4.11) and the latter part of paragraph (f) which seeks to prohibit terms which allow sellers or suppliers to retain sums for services not yet supplied where the seller or supplier dissolves the contract (*see* para 4.12).

# 6. High compensation clauses

(e)   *requiring any consumer who fails to fulfil his obligation to* **4.11**
     *pay a disproportionately high sum in compensation*

As already stated, this paragraph overlaps with paragraph (d) and the latter part of paragraph (f). It does, however, seek to regulate circumstances in which the seller or supplier may legitimately obtain compensation from the contracting consumer. In such circumstances, the level of compensation must not be a "disproportionately high sum". As in other areas of the Annex, the key term in this provision – "disproportionate" – is not defined. As a result, variation in the regulation of compensation clauses may continue between Member States. There are no examples of what may or may not be disproportionate compensation and perhaps a formula for calculating a maximum sum for compensation would have been of assistance.

## 7. **Unilateral dissolution and retention of sums provisions**

**4.12**  (f)  *authorising the seller or supplier to dissolve the contract on a discretionary basis where the same facility is not granted to the consumer, or permitting the seller or supplier to retain the sums paid for services not yet supplied by him where it is the seller or supplier himself who dissolves the contract*

The first part of paragraph (f) is likely to have a major effect on all contractual terms which allow the seller or supplier to dissolve the contract where the consumer does not have the same right. This will have a particular impact on contracts for the hire of consumer electronic goods where it is standard practice to allow the seller or supplier to dissolve the contract at any time, but where the consumer is required to guarantee a fixed term. Such terms will, in all probability, fail the test of fairness and thus will become invalid with the effect of locking the seller or supplier into the same fixed term as the consumer and of preventing the seller relying on any minimum term. A seller or supplier will only be allowed to rely upon such terms where the contract provides the consumer with an identical right to dissolve the contract on a discretionary basis. It will be up to sellers and suppliers to decide whether to exclude such terms from consumer contracts altogether or retain the right but suffer the risk that the consumer, relying on identical facilities, may dissolve the contract prior to the ending of any fixed term.

**4.13**    The latter part of this paragraph overlaps with paragraph (d) of the Annex which seeks to prohibit retention of part payment or deposit clauses and paragraph (e) which aims to preclude sellers and suppliers from relying upon disproportionately high compensation clauses. It should be noted that this section applies only in the event of the seller or supplier retaining sums paid for services not yet supplied. No provision is made for the return of sums paid for associated goods that have not been supplied to the consumer. Considered in conjunction with paragraphs (d) and (e), however, the cumulative effect of the Annex provisions in this area should provide the consumer with adequate protection.

## 8. **Termination without notice clauses**

**4.14**  (g)  *enabling the seller or supplier to terminate a contract of indeterminate duration without reasonable notice except where there are serious grounds for doing so*

As with other paragraphs of the Annex, paragraph (g) does not seek an absolute prohibition of termination without notice clauses, rather it seeks to prohibit termination clauses which do not provide "reasonable notice except where there are serious grounds for doing so". The Annex does not define what a reasonable notice period is, nor does it attempt to define what circumstances would amount to grounds serious enough to justify termination without notice. As a result it is possible that Member States will continue to vary in their approach to the regulation of termination without notice clauses.

Section 2 of the Annex limits the prohibition of "termination   **4.15** without notice" terms in respect of the supply of financial services. It states that "subparagraph (g) is without hindrance to terms by which a supplier of financial services reserves the right to terminate unilaterally a contract of indeterminate duration without notice where there is a valid reason, provided that the supplier is required to inform the other contracting party or parties thereof immediately". It is unclear whether a supplier terminating a financial services contract without notice merely has to inform the other party or parties of the fact of termination or of the reason for the termination as well. If a valid reason has to be given, it will require fundamental alterations in the policies of many financial institutions in respect of, for example, the management and termination of overdraft and lending facilities. Moreover, as a "valid reason" is not defined, there will be increased uncertainty amongst financial institutions as to what may or may not constitute acceptable grounds for invoking termination without notice clauses.

Section 2 prohibits the application of "termination without   **4.16** notice" clauses in respect of testing the fairness of contracts for the following financial services:

- transactions in transferable securities, financial instruments and other products or services where the price is linked to fluctuations in a stock exchange quotation or index or a financial market rate that the seller or supplier does not control;
- contracts for the purchase or sale of foreign currency, traveller's cheques or international money orders denominated in foreign currency.

Financial markets are often subject to massive price fluctuations within very short time spans. The above absolute limitation on the prohibition of termination without notice clauses can therefore be viewed as a commercial necessity and a recognition of the fact that it would be unrealistic and extremely cumbersome to operate such markets in accordance with paragraph (g) of the Annex.

## 9. **Unilateral extension of fixed duration contracts**

**4.17** (h) *automatically extending a contract of fixed duration where the consumer does not indicate otherwise, when the deadline fixed for the consumer to express this desire not to extend the contract is unreasonably early*

This provision recognises that consumers are often left unprotected when contracts require long periods of notice for discontinuance and where, in the absence of a notice of discontinuance, the contract automatically extend the original period. Such provisions exist in many contracts such as long-term car hire agreements, leasing of televisions, video machines and mobile phones, and service and maintenance contracts. The Directive recognises that most consumers only address their minds to the question of renewal in the period immediately before expiry of the original fixed contract or at purchase. In many cases, paragraph (h) will act as an incentive upon the supplier to remind the consumer of his/her right to opt for non-renewal of the fixed term and of extending the period during which the consumer can decide whether or not to renew the contract until very close to the renewal date. The Directive will thus introduce a test of fairness into the renewal period for contracts. Where it is probable that the consumer will only address the issue of renewal in the period immediately before the contract expires and the contract terms specify that the contract is deemed to be extended or a penalty clause has become operational because of late notice of renewal or non-renewal, then the provision is likely to be deemed unfair.

## 10. **Unseen terms**

**4.18** (i) *irrevocably binding the consumer to terms with which he had no real opportunity of becoming acquainted before the conclusion of the contract*

Arguably, this is the most important type of term that the Annex indicates should be construed as unfair. It certainly means that contractual terms that the consumer has not been made aware of will not be binding. Moreover, merely showing the consumer the terms of the contract will not necessarily suffice; the consumer must have a "real opportunity of becoming acquainted" with the terms of the contract. This terminology indicates that the consumer must have a realistic chance of understanding the implications of what he is binding himself to.

In certain circumstances, merely allowing the consumer to read **4.19** the contract will be adequate whilst in other situations the effect of the terms of the contract will have to be explained to the consumer, either by the seller or supplier directly or by the consumer being given the opportunity to take independent legal advice. The appropriate course of action will depend upon the length and complexity of the contract, the intelligibility of its terms and the ability of the consumer to understand those terms.

Where sellers and suppliers have to rely on complex contractual terms, time and date stamping of both the application form and contractual terms should provide added protection as it acts as evidence of the opportunity provided to the consumer to become acquainted with the terms of the contract. Use of such stamps to record the opportunity when the contract was actually entered into have been standard practice for many years within the banking industries of various Member States.

The requirements of this paragraph of the Annex should act as **4.20** an added incentive upon sellers and suppliers to ensure that the terms of their consumer contracts are intelligible and therefore easily understandable and should also act to deter sellers and suppliers from using pressure tactics to persuade consumers to enter into contracts. Consumers who have been subjected to such tactics may have grounds to argue that they have not had a real opportunity to become acquainted with the terms of the contract.

The provisions of this paragraph are wide enough to cover contracts involving the provision of instant credit. Its effect may be to deter such contractual arrangements except where the customer can be taken through the terms of the contract without feeling pressurised and with sufficiently clear explanations to ensure he/she understands the terms entered into. In some circumstances it may be advisable to provide contracting consumers with a cooling-off period, even where such a provision is not required by national statute.

Indirectly, paragraph (i) will place a requirement upon the **4.21** seller or supplier to assess the ability of the consumer to under-stand the contract that he or she is entering into. This is a concept which will be wholly novel to the consumer law of many Member States and it will be interesting to observe how the courts deal with this particular requirement.

## 11. **Unilateral alteration clauses**

**4.22** (j) *enabling the seller or supplier to alter the terms of the contract unilaterally without a valid reason which is specified in the contract*

In addition to outlawing unilateral non-performance and unilateral compensation or deposit clauses, the Directive also seeks to prevent the terms of the contract being changed without a valid reason. The Directive fails to provide guidelines as to what constitutes a valid reason, thereby creating another area of uncertainty. Paragraph (j), however, provides that if a seller or supplier is to rely successfully upon any reason for a unilateral alteration of contractual terms that reason must have already been identified in the contract, presumably at the time it was entered into. This provision will place a considerable burden upon sellers and suppliers in the drafting of their consumer contracts as they will have to identify in advance any reasons for unilateral alteration that they may rely upon.

**4.23** The final form of the Directive did not encompass the recommendations of the European Parliament that the consumer be protected from the seller or supplier reinterpreting the terms of the contract unilaterally by giving an unreasonably short period of notice. It is, however, submitted that if a seller or supplier should wish to rely upon such a term it is then open to the consumer to oppose it on the grounds that the effect of the reinterpretation is a unilateral alteration of the contractual terms. This is yet another area where there is scope for extensive litigation as a result of the failure clearly to define the prohibition that the Directive sought to achieve. The European Parliament also recommended that the seller or supplier be permitted to make alterations in the contract as a result of technical developments where this did not result in an increase in price or reduction in quality. This latter suggestion was not implemented. It is arguable, however, that the provision would have been otiose because any technical development is likely to be an improvement in the product or service which the customer would not complain about and similarly any reduction in quality or increase in price would breach the original contract agreed.

Paragraph 2(b) of the Annex allows a seller or supplier **4.24** contractually to reserve the right unilaterally to alter the conditions of contracts which are of indeterminate duration, notwithstanding the provisions of paragraph (j), so long as the seller or supplier is required to provide the consumer with reasonable notice of the change and, where the seller or supplier does alter the conditions, the consumer is free to dissolve the contract. "Reasonable notice" is not defined in the Annex. This provision may have major implications for contracts which run for an initial period and continue after that period ends until notice is given. In most consumer electronic hire arrangements, for example, the contracts are for indefinite periods. Thus any unilateral change of conditions will permit the consumer to dissolve the contract, even when the alteration and subsequent dissolution occur during the initial period of the contract.

The application of this paragraph is subject to a specific **4.25** restriction in respect of financial services. Paragraph 2(b) of the Annex provides that whenever any form of financial instrument or transaction is involved and there is a valid reason, the supplier will be able to change the rate of interest payable by the consumer or due to the consumer or the amount of charges for financial services without notice. The consumer, however, must be informed at the earliest opportunity of the change and must then be allowed the option of dissolving the contract. This provision has potential implications which are not immediately obvious. Where standard financing charges or interest rates on credit accounts have been determined by financial institutions in advance, for example, the "earliest opportunity" could mean that the consumer must be notified before the change comes into effect. As a result, the competitive advantages of late announce-ment of price changes may be lost to financial institutions. It would appear that the consumer will be able to insist on the reason for the change which must be a valid reason and in some cases may give rise to breach of contract actions.

Credit providers should be particularly aware that a consumer **4.26** will need to be free to dissolve the contract immediately upon being informed of a unilateral alteration of the contractual terms. Where a credit provider changes its terms, such as the basis for charging, the consumer will need to be free under the contract to withdraw his or her money without penalty and move to another financial institution. Any clause under the contract which imposes withdrawal or account closing fees is likely to be deemed void and unenforceable where the consumer purports to close his/her account as a result of notification by the provider that terms are to be changed.

Paragraph (j) does not apply to transactions in transferable securities, financial instruments and other products or services where prices fluctuate because they are linked to a stock exchange quotation, index or financial market rate which is not controlled by the supplier.

## 12. **Characteristics of unilateral alteration clauses**

**4.27**  (k)  *enabling the seller or supplier to alter unilaterally without a valid reason any characteristics of the product or service to be provided*

This paragraph overlaps to a considerable degree with paragraph (j) which seeks to prohibit unilateral alteration of contractual terms by the seller or supplier. In many cases the characteristics of the product or service will be a term of the contract and therefore both paragraphs (j) and (k) will be applicable.

**4.28**  As with paragraph (j), paragraph (k) does not absolutely prohibit unilateral alteration, rather it prohibits such alteration without a valid reason. Yet again the term "valid reason" is not defined and remains open to interpretation. Unlike paragraph (j), however, potential valid reasons do not have to be specified in the contract. Thus a seller or supplier may be able to rely upon previously unidentified reasons for unilaterally altering the characteristics of the product or service whereas he or she would not be able to do so in respect of unilateral alterations to contractual terms.

## 13. **Unilateral price imposition**

**4.29**  (l)  *providing for the price of goods to be determined at the time of delivery or allowing a seller of goods or supplier of services* *to increase their price without in both cases giving the consumer the corresponding right to cancel the contract if the final price is too high in relation to the price agreed when the contract was concluded*

The prohibition on determining the price of goods at the time of delivery will have profound consequences for many of the commercial operations dealing with consumers. In many cases, standard terms allow orders to be taken when goods are not in stock for a future delivery date and for any factory gate price increases to be passed on to consumers. Such clauses will now be viewed, at least initially, as unfair. The onus will be upon the vendor to show that it was fair to pass the price increases on to the consumer. In the majority of such cases it is probable that this will be a difficult burden to overcome, particularly when the contracting consumer is of the opinion that he or she had a fixed price contract.

The prohibition on determining the price of goods at the time of **4.30** delivery under paragraph (l) does not apply to the provision of services to the consumer. This limitation recognises the fact that the majority of services, from accountancy to plumbing, cannot always be adequately priced prior to the service being provided as it is often impossible to determine in advance the amount of work involved in providing the service.

Clauses entitling sellers or suppliers to increase their prices will **4.31** remain valid where the consumer has the right to terminate the contract without penalty where the price rise is too high in relation to the price originally agreed. The Directive again fails to provide a definition for the key term, "too high", thereby creating another area of uncertainty. It is possible that the different national courts will vary in the percentage price rise that is acceptable before the consumer has the right to break the contract. There is likely to be extensive litigation to determine what price rises are too high. In addition, it is open to consumers to claim that any price rise is too high and that the contract should be construed in their favour so that price rises are voided and/or the contract voided. One possible method by which sellers or suppliers may avoid this risk of litigation is to incorporate into contracts where prices are determinable at a future date clauses which specify a maximum possible rise in price.

This paragraph does not apply to any clause which allows **4.32** price-indexation, providing the method of indexation is precisely described, and will specifically not apply to transactions in transferable securities, financial instruments and other products or services where prices fluctuate because they are linked to a stock exchange quotation, index or financial market rate which is not controlled by the supplier.

## 14. Unilateral interpretation clauses

**4.33**   (m)   *giving the seller or supplier the right to determine whether the goods or services supplied are in conformity with the contract, or giving him the exclusive right to interpret any term of the contract*

Clauses allowing sellers or suppliers to determine whether the goods or services they supply are in conformity with the contract or entitling them exclusively to interpret contractual terms are not unusual in standard term consumer contracts. They are particularly prevalent in contracts relied upon by builders and property developers. In the past, such terms have enabled commercial undertakings to escape liability where the goods or services varied to a moderate degree from original specifications. The fact that after implementation sellers and suppliers will no longer be able to rely upon such unilateral interpretation clauses is likely to have a serious impact on those organisations accustomed to using such terms, particularly as paragraph (m) does not permit reliance upon such terms even where there is a "valid reason" to do so.

**4.34**   Paragraph (m) substantially overlaps with paragraphs (f), (j), (k), (l) and (o). Considered as a whole, they should be effective in ensuring that any term in a consumer contract which purports to permit a seller or supplier to alter the contract on a unilateral basis to the detriment of the contracting consumer shall be deemed unfair.

## 15. Agency and formality requirements

**4.35**   (n)   *limiting the seller's or supplier's obligation to respect commitments undertaken by his agents or making his commitments subject to compliance with a particular formality*

The provisions on commitments undertaken by agents needs to be read in conjunction with the Directive on Self-Employed

Commercial Agents and their Obligations (OJ 1986 L382 at page 17). The purpose of this Directive is to streamline the duties and obligations between commercial agents and their principals.

Under the Unfair Terms in Consumer Contracts Directive, where **4.36** agents are used, whether self-employed agents or employed agents, the principal will no longer be able to plead lack of capacity or authority by his or her agent. Thus common exclusion clauses which state that "the Principal will not be bound by contractual changes made by his agent" will probably be adjudged void.

Paragraph (n) will be of particular interest to insurance **4.37** companies and other financial institutions as it will bind them to their agents' undertakings as to how the policy will operate. Where, for example, the agent states that a mortgage protection policy will protect the mortgagor in the event of unemployment, the new rules on agency may create estoppel (via the agent) against the insurer seeking an indemnity for monies paid under the policy of the mortgage. Similarly, where a principal attempts to avoid such responsibilities by requiring his/her agent to make all arrangements subject to later approval or avoiding a change in the contractual terms made by the agent by requiring any changes to be made in writing by the principal then there is a strong possibility that the term will fail the fairness test and the principal will be bound by the agent's changes. This will potentially have serious implications for insurance companies where the agents make representations about the returns available at the end of the policy, about the operation of the policy, renewal or early encashment terms, as the effect of paragraph (n) on these representations will be that the insurers are bound because the term limiting the principal's liability will become invalid. There will also be implications in the fields of hire purchase and other financing arrangements where the agent will now be able to make a binding change to the policy conditions.

## 16. **Unilateral obligations clauses**

(o)  *obliging the consumer to fulfil all his obligations where the* **4.38**
     *seller or supplier does not perform his*

This provision overlaps with and is the corollary of the provisions under paragraphs (b), (c) and (j) to (l) because the effect of not binding a seller or supplier to his or her contractual obligations is to enable unilateral change by that seller or supplier. Contractual terms which enable sellers and suppliers to avoid their obligations, whilst not providing a similar right to the contracting consumer, are quite obviously unfair and are unlikely to withstand judicial scrutiny whether considered under this Directive or other EU or national laws.

## 17. **Transfer of rights clauses**

**4.39**   (p)   *giving the seller or supplier the possibility of transferring his rights and obligations under the contract, where this may serve to reduce the guarantees for the consumer, without the latter's agreement*

Paragraph (p) relates to clauses permitting assignment of the contract by the seller or supplier to a third party. It must be noted that paragraph (p) does not seek to prohibit assignment clauses, indeed, in the vast majority of cases, it does not seek to take any action against such clauses whatsoever. It is only if the assignment to a third party reduces the guarantees enjoyed by the contracting consumer and only if the contracting consumer does not agree to this course of action that paragraph (p) indicates that such clauses should be considered unfair. Given the limited nature of paragraph (p), it is unlikely to have any substantial impact on assignment clauses in consumer contracts.

## 18. **Restrictions on legal remedies**

**4.40**   (q)   *excluding or hindering the consumer's right to take legal action or exercise any other legal remedy, particularly by requiring the consumer to take disputes to arbitration not covered by legal provisions, unduly restricting the evidence available to him or imposing on him a burden of proof which, according to the applicable law, should lie with another party to the contract*

**4.41**   Other sections of the Annex, in particular paragraph (b), attempt to prohibit clauses that would limit or exclude legal rights that would otherwise be available to the consumer. Paragraph (q) concentrates upon clauses that seek to limit a consumer's legal rights in the event of that party seeking to commence or having actually commenced litigation against the seller or supplier. Certainly a contractual term that precludes the right to take legal action in any form should be deemed unfair. Paragraph (q), however, goes further. Arbitration clauses, for example, should also be deemed unfair when the arbitration body is not covered by legal provisions. This is not a blanket prohibition against arbitration clauses and it remains unclear whether the Directive intends to prohibit such clauses in the event that the arbitration body in question is completely unregulated or only partially so. Paragraph (q) also provides examples of clauses that are likely to be construed as unfair where they purport to influence procedural matters relating to litigation between the parties. Thus clauses restricting the use of evidence that would otherwise be available to the consumer will be invalid. In addition, paragraph (q) identifies as unfair clauses where sellers or suppliers seek to reverse the legal burden of proof to their own advantage. This latter provision is of particular importance given that the main body of the Directive creates, in most Member States, new burdens of proof which favour the consumer. Thus sellers and suppliers will not be able to contract out of the burden of proof placed upon them by Article 3 of the Directive should they wish to argue that the contract in question had been individually negotiated.

## 19. Conclusion

It must be emphasised, yet again, that the Directive's Annex of **4.42** unfair terms is of indicative value only. The relevant judicial and administrative bodies do not necessarily have to adjudge terms falling within the Annex as unfair and invalid. Moreover, many of the terms specified in the Annex need not be considered unfair on an absolute basis but will be permitted where there is a "valid reason", "reasonable notice" and the like. Such "buffer" provisions in the Annex are almost uniformly undefined, with the result that there will be considerable uncertainty as to what terms are or are not fair. These limitations, however, should be considered in the context of the limited approach to harmonisation that the Directive adopts.

Despite the above shortcomings, the Annex of unfair terms is **4.43** likely to be of great importance in the Directive's implementation.

Certain common approaches can be seen in its provisions, with a strong emphasis on the control of terms permitting unilateral decisions/actions on the part of sellers or suppliers and on clauses purporting to limit the legal rights of consumers. It will be interesting to observe the extent to which judicial and administrative bodies throughout the Union rely upon the Annex when it comes to the implementation of the Unfair Terms in Consumer Contracts Directive.

# Chapter 5
# UK Implementation

## 1. Introduction

Following the adoption of the Unfair Terms in Consumer Contracts **5.1**
Directive (93/13/EEC) (the Directive), the UK's Department of
Trade and Industry (DTI) proposed to implement its provisions by
introducing Regulations under section 2(2) of the European
Communities Act 1972. The DTI produced two consultation
documents on this subject, the first in October 1993 and the second
in 1994. The publication of the latter was due primarily to the high
level of response to the former. In December 1994 the proposed
measures were laid before Parliament and adopted as the Unfair
Terms in Consumer Contracts Regulations 1994 (SI 1994/3159)
("the Regulations"). Whilst, as a whole, the UK measures follow the
provisions of the Directive closely, there are certain deviations,
notably with regard to the implementation date and the ability of
consumer associations to take preventative action against unfair
terms. Of particular interest is the DTI's overall approach to the
prevention of continued use of unfair terms. This chapter examines
the proposed UK Regulations in the context of the development of
consumer protection in UK contract law.

## 2. UK regulation of contractual terms: the Unfair Contract Terms Act 1977

As has already been stated (*see* para **2.3** *supra*), the European **5.2**
Union's first Consumer Protection Programme in 1974 produced a
flurry of legislative responses by national governments in
individual Member States. In the UK the result was the Unfair
Contract Terms Act 1977 (UCTA 1977). The title of the Act is
something of a misnomer as the legislation does not attempt to
regulate unfair terms generally, concentrating attention mainly on
exemption clauses which attempt to exclude or limit liability
(analogous to subparagraph (a) of the Directive's indicative Annex

of Unfair Terms). The Act's approach to the regulation of exemption clauses is complex. Essentially, there are three areas of control: first, control over contractual terms exempting liability for negligence; secondly, control over clauses which exempt liability for breach of certain terms implied by statute or common law in contracts involving the sale, supply or hire-purchase of goods, which the Act renders absolutely ineffective; thirdly, there is a different form of control in respect of terms purporting to exclude or limit liability for breach of contract or which seek to enable one of the parties to perform their contractual obligations in a manner substantially different from that reasonably expected of him – such terms may be effective, but only in so far as the term satisfies the requirement of reasonableness. The Act defines this requirement of reasonableness as being "that the term shall have been a fair and reasonable one to be included having regard to the circumstances which were or ought reasonably to have been known to or in the contemplation of the parties when the contract is made" (s 11(1)).

## 3. The relationship between the Directive and UCTA 1977

**5.3**    There are similarities between UCTA 1977 and the Regulations. As a result, it has been argued that the Act and the Directive should be aligned by introducing a common test of fairness and by providing that the requirement of reasonableness under the Act should equate with the Directive's test of fairness. Whilst recognising the overlap between the legislation and accepting that it is likely, in many cases, that the test of fairness and the requirement of reasonableness will lead to similar results, the DTI has decided not to implement these proposals. The reason given for this approach is that the two tests are not the same and nor is the nature of the contractual terms which they cover. The Act deals mainly with exclusion clauses and, in certain circumstances, extends to contracts ·other than non-negotiated consumer contracts. The Directive, on the other hand, regulates only terms in consumer contracts, but is not limited to exclusion clauses.

**5.4**    Whilst implementation of the Directive will create a separate yet overlapping regime to that introduced by UCTA 1977, it is not proposed that the Act will be amended by the Directive's adoption in any way. Therefore, the protection provided by UCTA 1977 will remain. The DTI takes the view that the similarities between the two tests should alleviate any overlap arising between the two measures.

## 4. **Parties to the contract**

Regulation 2 provides the following definitions:      **5.5**

- "business" includes a trade or profession and the activities of any government department or local or public authority;
- "consumer" means a natural person who, in making a contract to which these Regulations apply, is acting for purposes which are outside his business;
- "seller" means a person who sells goods and who, in making a contract to which these Regulations apply, is acting for purposes relating to his business; and
- "supplier" means a person who supplies goods or services and who, in making a contract to which these Regulations apply, is acting for purposes relating to this business.

To all intents and purposes, these definitions correspond to those provided by the Directive (*see* para 2.3 supra). The DTI has taken care to ensure that the definition of consumer does not extend to partnerships and other unincorporated bodies.

## 5. **Exempted contracts**

Schedule 1 to the Regulations provides:      **5.6**

"The provisions of these Regulations do not apply to –
(a) any contract relating to employment;
(b) any contract relating to succession rights;
(c) any contract relating to rights under family law;
(d) any contract relating to the incorporation and organisation of companies or partnerships; and
(e) any term incorporated in order to comply with or which reflects –
(i) statutory or regulatory provisions of the United Kingdom; or
(ii) the provisions or principles of international conventions to which the Member States or the Community are party."

Schedule 1 to the Regulations mirrors the exemptions contained in      **5.7** the Preamble and Article 1(2) of the Directive; it does not go beyond that. In its first consultation document, the DTI proposed to exclude terms in contracts of insurance which define and circumscribe the insured risk and the insurer's liability. This was withdrawn in the amended proposals contained in the second consultation document. The DTI takes the view that such insurance terms, which are identified in the Directive's Preamble as terms to which the test of fairness should not apply (*see* para 3.5 supra), will be excluded under Regulation 3(2), which deals with the exemption of "core provisions" from the effects of the Regulations. The DTI make the valid point that by dealing with such insurance terms in this fashion the requirement of intelligibility will continue to apply.

**5.8**    It should be noted that the DTI takes the view that contractual terms not laid down by statute but which are agreed with a regulator established by statute and acting under powers derived ultimately from statute will fall outside the scope of the Regulations, under the exclusion contained in paragraph (e)(i) of Schedule 1.

## 6. **The test of fairness**

### (i)  **The definition of an individually negotiated term**

**5.9**    Regulation 3 identifies the terms to which the Regulations apply, stating:

> "(1) Subject to the provisions of Schedule 1, these Regulations apply to any term in a contract concluded between a seller or supplier and a consumer where the term has not been individually negotiated.
>
> (2) In so far as it is plain, intelligible language, no assessment shall be made of the fairness of any term which:
>
> (a) defines the main subject-matter of the contract, or
>
> (b) concerns the adequacy of the price or remuneration, as against the goods or services sold or supplied.
>
> (3) For the purposes of these Regulations, a term shall always be regarded as not having been individually negotiated where it has been drafted in advance, and the consumer has not been able to influence the substance of the term.
>
> (4) Notwithstanding that a specific term or certain aspects of it in a contract has been individually negotiated, these Regulations shall apply to the rest of a contract if an overall assessment of the contract indicates that it is a pre-formulated standard contract.
>
> (5) It shall be for any seller or supplier who claims that a term was individually negotiated to show that it was."

Regulation 3 follows the provisions of the Directive (*see* para 3.7 supra) up to and including the placement of the burden of proof upon the seller or supplier who wishes to argue that a term was individually negotiated.

Regulation 3(2) deals with the exclusion of terms relating to **5.10** subject matter and price/ratio from the test of fairness. This corresponds with the Directive's approach to such terms (*see* 3.14) which excludes such core provisions from the test of fairness whilst continuing to apply the requirement of intelligibility.

## (ii) **Factors determining fairness/unfairness**

The definition of an unfair term is contained in Regulation 4 and **5.11** Schedule 2:

"4(1) In these Regulations, subject to paragraph (2) and (3) below, 'unfair term' means any term which contrary to the requirement of good faith causes a significant imbalance in the parties' rights and obligations under the contract to the detriment of the consumer.

(2) An assessment of the unfair nature of a term shall be made taking into account the nature of the goods or services for which the contract was concluded and referring, as at the time of the conclusion of the contract, to all circumstances attending the conclusion of the contract and to all the other terms of the contract or of another contract on which it is dependent.

(3) In determining whether a term satisfies the requirement of good faith, regard shall be had in particular to the matters specified in Schedule 2 to these Regulations.

(4) Schedule 3 to these Regulations contains an indicative and non-exhaustive list of the terms which may be regarded as unfair.

SCHEDULE 2
ASSESSMENT OF GOOD FAITH

In making an assessment of good faith, regard shall be had in particular to:
– the strength of the bargaining positions of the parties,
– whether the consumer had an inducement to agree to the term,
– whether the goods or services were sold or supplied to the special order of the consumer, and
– the extent to which the seller or supplier has dealt fairly and equitably with the consumer."

**5.12**    The provisions of Regulations 4 and Schedule 2 reflect the contents of Articles 3 and 4 of the Directive, as well as the relevant recitals of the Preamble, but go no further. In particular, Schedule 2 to the Regulations, which identifies factors to be taken into consideration when making an assessment of good faith, does no more than reiterate the Directive's Preamble. Suggestions that additional factors, such as a reference to the conspicuousness and ease of understanding of the terms, as well as the extent to which the consumer had the benefit of independent legal advice, should be included in Schedule 2, have been rejected by the DTI. The DTI, in reaching this decision, made the point that Schedule 2 is not an exhaustive list and that matters such as these can be taken into account where appropriate.

**5.13**    The Directive's indicative Annex of Unfair Terms is incorporated into UK law under Regulation 4(4) and Schedule 3. The DTI rejected suggestions that the provisions of this indicative list should be strengthened, for example by reversing the burden of proof in favour of the consumer where such terms are in issue. The DTI takes the view that, even as an indicative list, the Annex is a helpful guide to those wishing to draw up contract terms and those who are considering challenging contract terms. For a detailed analysis of the Annex, see Chapter 4.

## 7. The requirement of intelligibility

**5.14**  Regulation 6 provides:

> "A seller or supplier shall ensure that any written term of a contract is expressed in plain, intelligible language, and if there is doubt about the meaning of a written term, the interpretation most favourable to the consumer shall prevail."

Regulation 6 mirrors the provisions of Article 5 of the Directive (*see* 3.17), including the provision that the interpretation of an ambiguous term most favourable to the consumer shall prevail. The DTI has taken the view that the requirement of intelligibility merely reflects the *contra proferentum* rule.

## 8. **The effect of unfair terms**

Regulation 5 states:                                            **5.15**

> "(1) An unfair term in a contract concluded with a consumer by a seller or supplier shall not be binding on the consumer.
> (2) The contract shall continue to bind the parties if it is capable of continuing in existence without the unfair term."

Regulation 5 is in line with the provisions of Article 6(1) of the Directive which renders unfair terms voidable (*see* 3.19).

## 9. **Contracts concluded in a non-Member State**

Regulation 7 states:                                            **5.16**

> "These Regulations shall apply notwithstanding any contract term which applies or purports to apply the law of a non-Member State, if the contract has a close connection with the territory of the Member States."

Regulation 7 corresponds with the relevant provisions of the Directive (*see* 3.21).

## 10. **Prevention of the continued use of unfair terms**

Under Article 7 of the Directive, Member States are placed under a **5.17** duty to make sure that "adequate and effective means exist" so that continued use of unfair terms is prevented. To this end, the Directive provides that persons or organisations having a legitimate interest under national law in protecting consumers may take action, under national law, before the courts or relevant administrative bodies to seek a determination as to whether contractual terms drawn up for general use are fair or unfair. Article 7 further provides that its legal remedies may be directed either separately or jointly against a number of sellers or suppliers from the same economic sector or their associations. In response to Article 7, the DTI has introduced Regulation 8, which states:

"(1) It shall be the duty of the Director (the Director General of Fair Trading) to consider any complaint made to him that any contract term drawn up for general use is unfair, unless the complaint appears to the Director to be frivolous or vexatious.

(2) If having considered a complaint about any contract term pursuant to paragraph (1) above the Director considers that the contract term is unfair he may, if he considers it appropriate to do so, bring proceedings for an injunction (in which proceedings he may also apply for an interlocutory injunction) against any person appearing to him to be using or recommending use of such a term in contracts concluded with consumers.

(3) The Director may, if he considers it appropriate to do so, have regard to any undertakings given to him by or on behalf of any person as to the continued use of such a term in contracts concluded with consumers.

(4) The Director shall give reasons for his decision to apply or not to apply, as the case may be, for an injunction in relation to any complaint which these Regulations require him to consider.

(5) The court on an application by the Director may grant an injunction on such terms as it thinks fit.

(6) An injunction may relate not only to use of a particular contract term drawn up for general use but to any similar term, or a term having like effect, used or recommended for use by any party to the proceedings.

(7) The Director may arrange for the dissemination in such form and manner as he considers appropriate of such information and advice concerning the operation of these Regulations as may appear to him to be expedient to give to the public and to all persons likely to be affected by these Regulations."

**5.18**    In its first consultation document, the DTI concluded that no action was necessary in the United Kingdom to implement the provisions of Article 7 of the Directive. This position drew a strong response. Business, as a whole, welcomed the DTI's approach whilst consumer groups, not surprisingly, opposed it. The DTI also received a substantial response from independent lawyers who argued that some form of implementation was required. As a result of these responses, the DTI has incorporated Regulation 8 into the proposed Regulations.

Regulation 8 would appear to offer a relatively simple and cost-effective method for the consumer to take action against unfair terms in consumer contracts. Essentially, it bypasses the need for the consumer to take direct legal action against the seller or supplier involved; instead, the consumer has merely to make a complaint to the Director General of Fair Trading (the Director). Once the Director is in receipt of such a complaint he is obliged to consider it unless it appears to be frivolous or vexatious. Unfortunately the terms "frivolous" and "vexatious" are not defined in the Regulations.

If, after considering the term in question, the Director is of the **5.19** opinion that the term is unfair, he *may*, if he considers it appropriate to do so, take legal action to bring an injunction against any person appearing to him to be using or recommending the use of such terms in consumer contracts. In considering whether to take legal action, the Director is obliged to take into consideration any undertakings given to him as to the continued use of the term or terms in question by any person. Such an undertaking may be made by the seller or supplier directly involved or by trade associations representing sellers or suppliers. This provision introduces a considerable degree of flexibility into the process to be adopted for the prevention of the continued use of unfair terms. Should the Director give a clear indication that he considers the term in question to be unfair, it is probable that in the majority of cases the offending sellers, suppliers or associations thereof will concede the future use of such terms, by way of undertaking, rather than face costly litigation.

A further positive aspect of Regulation 8 is the introduction of **5.20** transparency into the Director's decision-making process. Thus, the Director is obliged, whether or not he applies for an injunction, to give reasons for his decision.

As stated, the proposed UK approach to the prevention of the **5.21** continued use of unfair terms is a very positive one. Under the present litigious system for challenging such contractual terms, the vast majority of consumers are deterred from taking action by the high level of legal costs involved. A simple complaint to an administrative body, such as the Office of Fair Trading, who may or may not then take legal action, removes the issue of costs, and therefore removes a very strong deterrent in the effective enforcement of consumer legislation. The flexibility of this approach, with the potential use of undertakings by offending sellers and suppliers and the requirement upon the Director to provide reasons for his decisions in respect of individual complaints, is also to be welcomed.

One point upon which Regulation 8 may be criticised is on the **5.22** ground that there is no specific right of appeal from the decision of the Director. It would appear, therefore, that if the Director decides not to take any action in respect of a particular term or type of term, the complainant consumer is not in a position to take any further action. It is probable, however, that such decisions by the Director will be susceptible to judicial review, not least because the aggrieved complainant will be entitled to have a copy of the Director's reasons for the decision in question.

**5.23**  An important limitation in Regulation 8 is the failure to empower consumer organisations to challenge contractual terms generally in the courts. This is despite the fact that Article 7(2) of the Directive empowers organisations having a legitimate interest under national law in protecting consumers to take action. The DTI takes the view that since, at present, there is no general right of representative action in UK law, it is not appropriate or necessary to introduce such a right. It would appear, however, that the DTI's position on this point would not preclude consumer organisations from making a complaint to the Director under Regulation 8(1), which provides that the Director should consider *any complaint* made to him. If this is the correct interpretation of Regulation 8, then the failure to provide consumer organisations with a direct right of access to the courts in this area of law is removed.


# 11. **Implementation**


**5.24**  Under Article 10 of the Directive, Member States are required to implement the provisions of the Directive no later than 31 December 1994. The UK Regulations come into force on 1 July 1995, six months after the EU's identified implementation date. Whilst this is understandable given the very tight timetable involved in the adoption of the Directive and its ancillary implementation date in individual Member States, it is doubtful that this deviation from the provisions of the Directive would stand up to scrutiny under EU law. It remains to be seen whether there will be any challenges to allegedly unfair terms in consumer contracts between the EU and UK implementation dates.

# 12. **Conclusion**

As this chapter has made clear, most of the rules contained in the **5.25** proposed UK Regulations closely reflect the provisions of the Unfair Terms in Consumer Contracts Directive. The major exception, of course, are the proposed rules for the enforcement of the Regulations. Regulation 8 should ensure that, for the first time in the United Kingdom, the ordinary individual may be able to take rapid, efficient and inexpensive action to ensure that unfair terms in consumer contracts do not continue to be used. Such enforcement measures possess the potential to revolutionise the methods by which standard term consumer contracts are drafted and relied upon by sellers and suppliers, and will provide one of the strongest structures for consumer protection within the UK regulatory framework.

# *Appendix 1*

# Council Resolution

of 14 April 1975
on a preliminary programme of the European Economic
Community for a consumer protection and information policy

**AI.1** THE COUNCIL OF THE EUROPEAN COMMUNITIES,

Having regard to the Treaty establishing the European Economic Community;

Having regard to the communication from the Commission on the preliminary programme of the European Economic Community for consumer information and protection;

Having regard to the Opinion of the European Parliament[1];

Having regard to the Opinion of the Economic and Social Committee[2];

Whereas, pursuant to Article 2 of the Treaty, the task of the European Economic Community is to promote throughout the Community a harmonious development of economic activities, a continuous and balanced expansion and an accelerated raising of the standard of living;

Whereas the improvement of the quality of life is one of the tasks of the Community and as such implies protecting the health, safety and economic interests of the consumer;

Whereas fulfilment of this task requires a consumer protection and information policy to be implemented at Community level;

Whereas the Heads of State or of Government meeting in Paris on 19 and 20 October 1972 confirmed this requirement by calling upon the institutions of the Communities to strengthen and co-ordinate measures for consumer protection and to submit a programme by January 1974;

APPROVES the principle of a consumer protection and information policy and the principles, objectives and general description of action to be taken at Community level as set out in the preliminary programme annexed hereto; **AI.2**

NOTES that the Commission will at a later date submit suitable proposals for the implementation of this programme, using the ways and means mentioned therein; **AI.3**

UNDERTAKES to act on the above-mentioned proposals, if possible within nine months of the date on which they are forwarded by the Commission. **AI.4**

---

[1] OJ 1974 C62/8.
[2] OJ 1974 C97/47.

## Annex

## Preliminary Programme of the European Economic Community for a Consumer Protection and Information Policy

### Introduction

**A1.5**    1. The strengthening and co-ordination of action for consumer protection within the European Economic Community, aims which were emphasised by the Heads of State or of Government at the Paris summit conference in October 1972, constitute a manifest and widely felt need. The debate in the European Parliament on 20 September 1972, which stressed the need for a coherent and effective consumer protection policy, various subsequent statements made both in the Parliament and in the Economic and Social Committee, work already done in this field by the Community and the Member States and by several international organisations, particularly the Council of Europe and the OECD, bear witness to such a need.

The time has now come to implement a Community policy for consumer protection which, by marshalling, strengthening and supplementing the Community's work in this field, affirms its involvement in improving the quality of life of its peoples.

**A1.6**    2. The wide range of experience in the countries of the enlarged Community favours the development of new ideas in the consumer field which, together with the many developments which have taken place in all Member States, point the

way to a new deal for the consumer and ways to find a better balance in the protection of his interests.

3. The consumer is no longer seen    **A1.7**
merely as a purchaser and user of goods and services for personal, family or group purposes but also as a person concerned with the various facets of society which may affect him either directly or indirectly as a consumer. Consumer interests may be summed up by a statement of five basic rights:

(a) the right to protection of health and safety,

(b) the right to protection of economic interests,

(c) the right of redress,

(d) the right to information and education,

(e) the right of representation (the right to be heard).

4. All these rights should be given    **A1.8**
greater substance by action under specific Community policies such as the economic, common agricultural, social, environment, transport and energy policies as well as by the approximation of laws, all of which affect the consumer's position.

Such action falls within the context of a policy for improving the conditions of life in the Community.

5. This paper sets out the objectives    **A1.9**
and general principles of a consumer policy. It also sets out a number of

priority measures to be taken during the coming years. In such a large and developing field it seemed preferable to limit the amount of work in the initial phase, on the understanding that new guidelines could be evolved on proposals from the Commission as the programme progressed.

# I.  General Considerations

## A.  THE CONSUMER AND THE ECONOMY

**AI.10**  6.  While consumer protection has long been an established fact in the Member States of the Community, the concept of a consumer policy is relatively recent. It has developed in response to the abuses and frustrations arising at times from the increased abundance and complexity of goods and services afforded the consumer by an ever-widening market. Although such a market offers certain advantages, the consumer, in availing himself of the market, is no longer able properly to fulfil the role of a balancing factor. As market conditions have changed, the balance between suppliers and customers has tended to become weighted in favour of the supplier. The discovery of new materials, the introduction of new methods of manufacture, the development of means of communication, the expansion of markets, new methods of retailing – all these factors have had the effect of increasing the production, supply and demand of an immense variety of goods and services. This means that the consumer, in the past usually an individual purchaser in a small local market, has become merely a unit in a mass market, the target of advertising campaigns and of pressure by strongly organised production and distribution groups. Producers and distributors often have a greater opportunity to determine market conditions than the consumer. Mergers, cartels and certain self-imposed restrictions on competition have also created imbalances to the detriment of consumers.

7.  Trade practices, contractual **AI.II** terms, consumer credit and the very concept of competition itself have all developed.

Such changes have merely accentuated the abovementioned imbalances and made consumers and governments more aware of the need to keep the former better informed of their rights and protected against abuses which might arise from such practices.

Thus practices which were once regarded in many countries as unfair solely in terms of competition between producers (misleading advertising, for example), are now also considered from the point of view of relations between producers and consumers.

8.  Attempts have been made to **AI.I2** correct the imbalance of power between producers and consumers mentioned in paragraphs 6 and 7. Increasingly detailed information is therefore needed to enable consumers, as far as possible, to make better use of their resources, to have a freer choice between the various products or services offered and to influence prices and product and market trends. Thus studies, surveys and comparative tests have been

carried out on the quality and usefulness of products and services on price policy, market conditions, consumer behaviour and the rationalisation of work in the home etc.

**AI.13**  9.  Well aware that as individuals they have very little power, consumers are understandably trying to form organisations to protect their interests, and calls for greater consumer participation in decision-making have likewise become more numerous.

B.  THE EUROPEAN ECONOMIC COMMUNITY AND CONSUMERS

**AI.14**  10.  The preamble to the Treaty establishing the European Economic Community cites as one of the basic aims of the Community "the constant improvement of the living and working conditions" of the peoples constituting the Community. This idea is elaborated in Article 2 of the Treaty which includes among the tasks of the Community the promotion of "harmonious development of economic activities, a continuous and balanced expansion, an increase in stability, an accelerated raising of the standard of living".

To achieve this aim, a number of steps have already been taken in accordance with the form and means provided by the Treaty.

11.  Article 39 of the Treaty contains  **AI.15** a direct reference to consumers. It states that the objectives of the common agricultural policy include the guaranteed availability of supplies and the stabilisation of markets, and then mentions also the aim "to ensure that supplies reach consumers at reasonable prices".

12.  In dealing with rules on compe-  **AI.16** tition, Article 85 (3) of the Treaty makes authorisation for certain agreements between undertakings subject to the consumer receiving "a fair share" of the resulting benefit, while Article 86 gives as an example of unfair practices "limiting production, markets or technical development to the prejudice of consumers".

13.  Annex 1 contains a note of  **AI.17** action of interest to consumers taken by the Community so far.

Annex 2 contains a selection of Council Directives of interest to consumers.

Although the general Community policy is the outcome of a compromise between the conflicting economic interest and diverse policies of the Member States, it is apparent that progress has been made in consumer protection and information; however, further progress must still be made.

## II  Objectives of Community Policy Towards Consumers

**AI.18**  14.  Given the tasks assigned to the Community, it follows that all action taken has repercussions on the consumer. One of the Community's prime objectives, in general terms, is therefore to take full account of consumer interests in the various sectors of Community activity, and to

satisfy their collective and individual needs. Thus there would seem to be a need to formulate a specific Community consumer information and protection policy. In relation to the other common policies, such a policy would take the form of a general guideline aimed at improving the position of consumers whatever the production, distribution or service sector in question. The aims of such a policy are to secure:

A. effective protection against hazards to consumer health and safety,
B. effective protection against damage to consumers' economic interests,
C. adequate facilities for advice, help and redress,
D. consumer information and education,
E. consultation with and representation of consumers in the framing of decisions affecting their interests.

## A. PROTECTION OF CONSUMER HEALTH AND SAFETY

**AI.19** 15. Measures for achieving this objective should be based on the following principles:

### (a) Principles

(i) Goods and services offered to consumers must be such that, under normal or foreseeable conditions of use, they present no risk to the health or safety of consumers. There should be quick and simple procedures for withdrawing them from the market in the event of their presenting such risks.

In general, consumers should be informed in an appropriate manner of any risk liable to result from a foreseeable use of goods and services, taking account of the nature of the goods and services and of the persons for whom they are intended.

(ii) The consumer must be protected against the consequences of physical injury caused by defective products and services supplied by manufacturers of goods and providers of services.

(iii) Substances or preparations which may form part of or be added to foodstuffs should be defined and their use regulated, for example by endeavouring to draw up in Community rules, clear and precise positive lists. Any processing which foodstuffs may undergo should also be defined and their use regulated where this is required to protect the consumer.

Foodstuffs should not be adulterated or contaminated by packaging or other materials with which they come into contact, by their environment, by the conditions in which they are transported or stored or by persons coming into contact with them, in such a way that they affect the health or safety of consumers or otherwise become unfit for consumption.

(iv) Machines, appliances and electrical and electronic equipment and any other category of goods which may prejudicially affect the health and safety of consumers either in themselves or by their use, should be covered by special rules and be subject to a procedure recognised or approved by the public authorities (such as type approval or declaration of conformity with harmonised standards or rules) to ensure that they are safe for use.

(v) Certain categories of new products which may prejudicially affect the health or safety of consumers should be made subject to special authorisation procedures harmonised throughout the Community.

*(b) Priorities*

**Al.20** 16. In order to promote the free movement of goods, the Community is already actively pursuing a policy of approximation of laws in the agricultural, foodstuffs and industrial sectors. The Council has adopted several programmes[3] relating to specific fields, with a view to harmonising the provisions laid down by law, regulation or administrative action in the Member States. These programmes establish priority objectives for the approximation of legislation and a timetable for achieving them. The fields which are of special importance for the protection of the consumer's health and safety are the following:

– foodstuffs,
– cosmetics and detergents,
– utensils and consumer durables,
– cars,
– textiles,
– toys,
– dangerous substances,
– materials coming into contact with foodstuffs,
– medicines,
– fertilisers, pesticides and herbicides,
– veterinary products and animal feedingstuffs.[4]

17. In this field the Community will: **Al.21**

– implement the programmes referred to in paragraph 16, particularly as regards consumer priorities;
– continue to study the results of current research into substances which may affect the health or safety of consumers, as mentioned particularly in paragraph 16 and, if necessary, take steps to coordinate and encourage such research;
– determine those products or categories of products which, because of the hazards they present to health or safety, should be subject to harmonised authorisation procedures throughout the Community.

B. PROTECTION OF THE ECONOMIC INTERESTS OF THE CONSUMERS

18. This kind of protection should **Al.22** be ensured by laws and regulations which are either harmonised at Community level or adopted directly at that level and are based on the principles set out below.[4]

*(a) Principles*

19. (i) Purchasers of goods or **Al.23** services should be protected against the abuse of power by the seller, in particular against one-sided standard contracts[5], the unfair exclusion of essential

---

[3] General programme for the elimination of technical barriers to trade in industrial products and foodstuffs resulting from disparities between the provisions laid down by law, regulation or administrative provisions in the Member States, laid down by the Council Resolution of 28 May 1969 (JO 1969 C76) at p 1 and supplemented by the Council Resolution of 21 May 1973 (OJ 1973 C38) at p 1.
    Action programme of 17 December 1973 on industrial and technological policy (Council Resolution of 17 December 1973 (OJ 1973 C117) at p 1).
[4] Council Resolution of 22 July 1974 (OJ 1974 C92) at p 2.
[5] See para 48.

rights in contracts, harsh conditions of credit, demands for payment for unsolicited goods and against high-pressure selling methods.

(ii) The consumer should be protected against damage to his economic interests caused by defective products or unsatisfactory services.

(iii) The presentation and promotion of goods and services, including financial services, should not be designed to mislead, either directly or indirectly, the person to whom they are offered or by whom they have been requested.

(iv) No form of advertising – visual or aural – should mislead the potential buyer of the product or service. An advertiser in any medium should be able to justify, by appropriate means, the validity of any claims he makes.

(v) All information provided on labels at the point of sale or in advertisements must be accurate.

(vi) The consumer is entitled to reliable after-sales service for consumer durables including the provision of spare parts required to carry out repairs.

(vii) The range of goods available to consumers should be such that as far as possible consumers are offered an adequate choice.

*(b) Priorities*

**AI.24** 20. (i) *To harmonise the general conditions of consumer credit, including those relating to hire-purchase*

Studies carried out following the recent development of credit facilities show that the consumer needs help in this field.

21. On the basis of studies already **AI.25** carried out by its own departments and by national authorities, the Commission will submit proposals on the general conditions of consumer credit.

22. (ii) *To protect the consumer by* **AI.26** *appropriate measures against false or misleading advertising*:

– by establishing principles for assessing the extent to which an advertisement is false, misleading or generally unfair;

– by taking steps to prevent the consumer's economic interests from being harmed by false, misleading or unfair advertising;

– by studying methods of putting a rapid end to deceptive or misleading advertising campaigns and ensuring that advertisers' claims are valid;

– by studying the possibility of counteracting the effects of false or misleading advertising, for example by publishing corrective advertisements;

– by studying the problems arising in connection with reversal of the burden of proof.

23. To this end, the Commission **AI.27** will:

– build upon the work already done[6], supplementing it where necessary by specific studies;

– proceed with the work being done in connection with the harmonisation of laws;

– submit appropriate proposals to the Council.

24 (iii) *To protect consumers from* **AI.28**

---

[6] See para 48.

*unfair commercial practices*, for example in the following areas:

- terms of contracts[7];
- conditions in guarantees, particularly for consumer durables;
- door-to-door sales[7];
- premium offers;
- unsolicited goods and services;
- information given on labels and packaging etc.

**AI.29**  25. To this end, the Commission will:

- collate the measures already taken by the Member States and the studies already made or being made by international organisations;
- submit all appropriate proposals to the Council.

**AI.30**  26. (iv) *To harmonise the law on product liability so as to provide better protection for the consumer*

**AI.31**  27. To this end, the Commission will submit appropriate proposals to the Council on the basis of studies already carried out or in progress.[7]

**AI.32**  28. (v) *To improve the range and quality of services provided for consumers*

**AI.33**  29. In this complex and, for the most part, little-researched field, there is great scope for discussion and action on the part of the Community. The Commission will carry out a study in this area. It will report its conclusions before 31 December 1975 and, if appropriate, submit proposals.

30. (vi) *To promote the more general economic interests of consumers*

**AI.34**  In order better to satisfy the indi-

vidual and collective needs of consumers, solutions should be sought to certain general problems such as:

- how the individual can obtain better value for money for the goods and services supplied;
- how waste can be prevented, particularly as regards:
  - packaging,
  - the life of goods,
  - the recycling of materials;
- how protection can be provided against forms of advertising which encroach on the individual freedom of consumers.

31. Given that the concern for such **AI.35** matters is relatively recent, the Commission will endeavour to establish through research a basis for future action.

## C.  ADVICE, HELP AND REDRESS

### (a) Principles

32. Consumers should receive **AI.36** advice and help in respect of complaints and of injury or damage resulting from purchase or use of defective goods or unsatisfactory services.

Consumers are also entitled to proper redress for such injury or damage by means of swift, effective and inexpensive procedures.

### (b) Action

33. To this end, the Commission **AI.37** will:

(i)  study:
  - systems of assistance and advice in the Member States,

---

[7] See para 48.

- systems of redress, arbitration and the amicable settlement of disputes existing in the Member States,
- the laws of the Member States relating to consumer protection in the courts, particularly the various means of recourse and procedures, including actions brought by consumer associations or other bodies,
- systems and laws of the kind referred to above in certain third countries;

(ii) publish papers synthesising and comparing the advantages and disadvantages of the different systems, procedures and documentation relating to consumer assistance, advice and to redress and legal remedies;

(iii) submit, where necessary, appropriate proposals for improving the existing systems and putting them to better use;

(iv) study the feasibility of a procedure for exchanging information on the outcome of action for redress and legal recourse relating to products mass-marketed in all or several Member States.

### D. CONSUMER INFORMATION AND EDUCATION

#### Consumer information

##### (a) Principles

**AI.38** 34. Sufficient information should be made available to the purchaser of goods or services to enable him to:

- assess the basic features of the goods and services offered such as the nature, quality, quantity and price;
- make a rational choice between competing products and services;
- use these products and services safely and to his satisfaction;
- claim redress for any injury or damage resulting from the product supplied or service received.

##### (b) Priorities

35. (i) *Information concerning goods and services*

- to formulate general principles **AI.39** which should apply in the preparation of all specific directives and other rules relating to consumer protection;
- to lay down rules for the labelling of products for which specifications are harmonised at Community level. These rules should provide that all labelling must be clear, legible and unambiguous;
- for foodstuffs, to draw up rules stating clearly the particulars that should be given to the consumer (*e.g.* the nature, composition, weight or volume, the food value, the date of manufacture or any other useful date marking, etc);
- for products other than foodstuffs, and for services, to draw up rules stating clearly the particulars which are of interest to the consumer and which should be given to him;
- to draw up common principles for stating the price and possibly the price per unit of weight or volume;
- to encourage the use and harmonisation of systems of voluntary informative labelling.

36. (ii) *Comparative tests*

Comparative tests are another source **AI.40**

of information. Such tests may be carried out by state-financed bodies, private bodies or a combination of the two. These bodies would have much to gain from a co-ordinated exchange of information.[8]

The Commission will take the necessary steps to ensure that the bodies carrying out comparative tests in the Member States co-operate as closely as possible, particularly by conducting tests jointly and even by laying down similar standards for such tests.

37. (iii) *Study of consumer behaviour*

**A1.41** In order to establish an integrated policy on consumer information and education, more needs to be known about consumer behaviour and attitudes. The Commission already conducts regular consumer surveys on certain aspects of the Community's economic situation. It will continue these surveys and extend them to other subjects, in co-operation with Member States, consumer organisations and other bodies, so as to learn more about the needs and behaviour of consumers within the Community.

**A1.42** 38. (iv) To inform consumers in simple terms of measures taken at national and Community level which may directly or indirectly affect their interests.

**A1.43** 39. For the Commission, such action will comprise in particular:

- setting out the categories of consumer information about goods and services which are most needed for consumers in the Community and preparing documentation on that basis;

- providing an increasing amount and range of clear information on consumer matters being dealt with by the Community, in close co-operation with Member States and consumer and other organisations;
- encouraging the production of television and radio programmes and films and the publication of press articles etc, on consumer topics;
- publishing an annual report on steps taken by the Community and the Member States in the consumer interest by legislation and its implementation, information, consultation and co-ordination.

(v) *Information on prices*

40. Consumers should be informed **A1.44** of the factors determining prices within the Community.

Such information will be supplied by the Commission, particularly in the annual report mentioned in paragraph 39.

41. The Commission should con- **A1.45** tinue to carry out surveys of retail prices and endeavour to inform the public as soon as possible of price differences within the Community.

**Consumer education**

(a) *Principle*

42. Facilities should be made **A1.46** available to children as well as to young people and adults to educate them to act as discriminating consumers, capable of making an informed choice of goods and services and conscious of their rights

---

[8] See para 48.

and responsibilities. To this end, consumers should, in particular, benefit from basic information on the principles of modern economics.

### (b) Action

43. (i) *Promotion of consumer education*

**A1.47** In order to further the advance of consumer education by providing advice and opinions at Community level, the Commission should undertake further studies in co-operation with Member States and consumer organisations.

The object of such studies, carried out in conjunction with experts from the Member States, should be to determine methods and suggest materials for the encouragement of consumer education in the curricula of schools, universities and other educational establishments.

44. (ii) *Training the instructors*

**A1.48** Training those who are to instruct others is a necessary task on which a number of ideas have been advanced. For instance, centres could be set up in the Member States to provide such training, based on the results of economic and sociological research. Exchanges of ideas, of staff and of students between such centres have also been considered. The Commission will encourage work in this field.

45. (iii) *Dissemination of a wide range of information*

**A1.49** As part of its general information policy, the Commission will encourage the exchange and dissemination

of information on topics of interest to consumers, in co-operation with national authorities and bodies concerned with consumer affairs. Publication of the annual report referred to in paragraph 39 will also provide a means of increasing consumer awareness.

E.   CONSUMER CONSULTATION AND REPRESENTATION

### (a) Principles

46. When decisions which concern **A1.50** them are prepared, consumers should be consulted and allowed to express their views, in particular through organisations concerned with consumer protection and information.

### (b) Action

47. In this field, the Commission will:

(i)   carry out on the basis of existing **A1.51** studies[9] a comparative study of the different procedures for consumer consultation, representation and participation currently employed in the Member States and in particular the rules and criteria relating to how representative consumer organisations are and whether they are to be recognised by the authorities;

(ii)   encourage organisations representing consumers to study certain matters of particular importance for consumers, to make known their views and co-ordinate their efforts;

---

[9] See para 48.

(iii) promote exchanges of information between Member States on the most appropriate way of providing consumers with channels through which to be consulted or to express their views.

## III.   Implementation

**AI.52** 48.   In implementing its programme, the Commission will take full account of studies and other work already carried out by the Member States, international bodies[10] and consumer organisations, and will collaborate with them so as to enable the Community to take advantage of work already in progress.

In this context, co-operation with the Council of Europe and OECD is of particular importance in view of the work undertaken by these organisations on subjects relating to consumer protection and information.

The importance of such collaboration cannot be over-emphasised and everything possible will be done to maintain and develop the close links and harmonious relations already established or in the making in the field of consumer affairs.

49.   This text should be regarded as **AI.53** the first stage of a more comprehensive programme which might need to be developed at a later date. The aim is to complete this first stage within four years.

---

## Appendix I

### Action of Interest to Consumers Taken by the Community So Far

**AI.54** The development of the European Economic Community and the establishment of a customs union have been of interest to consumers particularly in the following areas:

(a)   *Widening of consumer choice*

Free movement of products has given consumers a wider choice and ensured more regular supplies.

(b)   *Competition and prices*

Application of Articles 85 and 86 of the Treaty has helped to maintain competition in the common market with the resultant effect on pricing.

(c)   *Harmonisation of rules*

The interests of consumers, particularly with regard to health and safety, have been taken into consideration in

---

[10] The bodies with which collaboration will be maintained include:
  – United Nations; United Nations Educational, Scientific and Cultural Organisation; World Health Organisation; Food and Agriculture Organisation and Codex Alimentarius; Organisation for Economic Co-operation and Development; Council of Europe; Nordic Committee on Consumer Matters;
  – International Standards Organisation and International Electrotechnical Commission, European Committee for Standardisation and European Committee for Electrotechnical Standardisation.

the drafting of several directives on agriculture and industrial products (examples are given in Annex 2).

(d) *Consumer information and representation*

Information made available by the information services of the Commission has been supplemented by a number of statements issued by the Consumers' Contact Committee which existed from 1962 to 1972.

The Commission has now established the Environment and Consumer Protection Service, one of the Divisions of which specialises in consumer information and protection.

To fill the gap left after the Contact Committee was disbanded, the Commission has set up a Consumers' Consultative Committee (Decision of 15 September 1973[11]), which met for the first time on 19 November 1973.

There are also a number of other Advisory Committees on which, in addition to consumers, producers and other interests are represented, particularly in the agricultural and customs sectors.

---

# Appendix 2

A Selection of Council Directives of Interest to Consumers (as at 31 May 1974)

FOODSTUFFS

**AI.55**  1.  *Authorised colouring matters*:

Approximation of rules:

Directive of 23 October 1962 (JO 1962 115) at 2645/62, as amended by Directive Nos:

– 65/469/EEC 1965 (JO 1965 L178) at p 2793/65;
– 67/653/EEC 1967 (JO 1967 263) at p 4;
– 68/419/EEC 1968 (JO 1968 L309) at p 24;
– 70/358/EEC 1970 (JO 1970 L157) at p 36.

**AI.56**  2.  *Authorised preservatives*:

(a)  Approximation of laws:

Directive No 64/54/EEC of 5 November 1963 (JO 1964 12) at p 161/64, as amended by Directive Nos:

– 65/66/EEC (JO 1965 22 ) at p 373/65;
– 66/722/EEC (JO 1966 233) at p 3947/66;
– 67/427/EEC (JO 1967 148) at p 1;
– 68/420/EEC (JO 1968 L309) at p 25;
– 70/359/EEC (JO 1970 L157) at p 38;
– 71/160/EEC (JO 1971 L87) at p 12;
– 72/2/EEC (JO 1972 L298) at p 48;
– 74/62/EEC (OJ 1974 L 38) at p 29.

(b)  Criteria of purity for authorised preservatives: Directive No 65/66/EEC of 26 January 1965 (JO 1965 22)

---

[11] OJ 1973 L283 at p 18.

at p 373/65, as amended by Directive No 67/428/EEC (JO 1967 148) at p 10, revision (JO 1965 126) at p 2148/65.

(c) Use and control measures for the qualitative and quantitative analysis of preservatives in and on fruit: Directive No 67/427/EEC of 27 June 1967 (JO 1967 148) at p 1.

3. *Authorised antioxidants in food-stuffs*:

Directive No 70/357/EEC of 13 July 1970 (JO 1970 L157) at p 31.

4. *Cocoa and chocolate products*:

Approximation of laws: Directive No 73/241/EEC of 24 July 1973 (OJ 1973 L288) at p 23.

5. *Sugar*:

Approximation of laws: Directive No 73/437/EEC of 11 December 1973 (OJ 1973 L356) at p 71.

VETERINARY DIRECTIVES

**A1.57** 1 *Directive on animal health problems affecting intra-Community trade in bovine animals and swine*:

Directive No 64/432/EEC of 26 June 1964 (JO 1964 121) at p 1977/64, as amended by Directive Nos:

– 66/600/EEC (JO 1966 192) at p 3294/66;
– 70/360/EEC (JO 1970 L157) at p 40;
– 71/285/EEC (JO 1971 L179) at p 1;
– 72/97/EEC (JO 1972 L38) at p 95;
– 72/445/EEC (JO 1972 L298) at p 49;
– 73/150/EEC (OJ 1973 L172) at p 18.

2. *Health problems affecting trade in fresh poultrymeat*:

Directive No 71/118/EEC of 15 February 1971 (JO 1971 L55) at p 23.

3 *Health problems affecting intra-Community trade in fresh meat*:

Directive No 64/433/EEC of 26 June 1964 (JO 1964 121) at p 2012/64), as amended by Directive Nos:

– 66/601/EEC (JO 1966 192) at p 3302/66;
– 69/349/EEC (JO 1969 L256) at p 5;
– 70/486/EEC (JO 1970 L239) at p 42.

ANIMAL NUTRITION

1 *Introduction of Community* **A1.58** *methods of sampling and analysis for the official control of feedingstuffs*:

Directive No 70/373/EEC of 20 July 1970 (JO 1970 L170) at p 1, as amended by Directive No 72/275/EEC (JO 1972 L171) at p 39.

2. *Additives in feedingstuffs*:

Directive No 70/524/EEC of 23 November 1970 (JO 1970 L270) at p 1, as amended by Directive No 73/103/EEC (OJ 1973 L124) at p 17.

3. *Undesirable substances and products in feedingstuffs*:

Directive No 74/63/EEC of 17 December 1973 (OJ 1974 L38) at p 31.

HEALTH PROTECTION

1. *Proprietary medicinal products*:   **A1.59**

Approximation of laws: Directive No 65/65/EEC of 26 January 1965 (JO 1965 22) at p 369/65, as amended by Directive No 66/454/EEC (JO 1966 144) at p 2658/66.

2. *Classification, packaging and labelling of dangerous substances*:

(a) Approximation of laws: Directive No 67/548/EEC of 27 June 1967 (JO 1967 196) at p 1, as amended by Directive Nos:
  – 70/189/EEC (JO 1970 L59) at p 33;
  – 71/144/EEC (JO 1971 L74) at p 15;
  – 73/146/EEC (OJ 1973 L167) at p 1.

(b) Classification, packaging and labelling of dangerous preparations (solvents): Directive No 73/173/EEC of 4 June 1973 (OJ 1973 189 ) at p 7.


TEXTILES

**A1.60** 1. *Textile names*:

Approximation of laws: Directive No 71/307/EEC of 26 July 1971 (JO 1971 L185) at p 16.

2. *Quantitative analysis of binary textile fibre mixtures*:

Approximation of laws: Directive No 72/276/EEC of 17 July 1972 (JO 1972 L173) at p 1.

3. *Quantitative analysis of ternary textile fibre mixtures*:

Approximation of laws: Directive No 73/44/EEC of 26 February 1973 (OJ 1973 L83) at p 1.


INDUSTRIAL PRODUCTS

**Detergents**

**A1.61** 1. *Detergents*:

Approximation of laws: Directive No 73/404/EEC of 22 November 1973 (OJ 1973 L347) at p 51.

2. *Methods of testing the biodegradability of anionic surfactants*:

Approximation of laws: Directive No 73/405/EEC of 22 November 1973 (OJ 1973 L347) at p 53.

**Crystal glass**

Description and labelling of crystal glass: Directive No 69/493/EEC of 15 December 1969 (JO 1969 L326) at p 36.

**Non-automatic weighing machines**

Approximation of laws: Directive No 73/360/EEC of 19 November 1973 (OJ 1973 L355) at p 1.

**Electrical equipment for use within certain voltage limits**

Approximation of laws: Directive No 73/23/EEC of 19 February 1973 (OJ 1973 L77) at p 29.


MOTOR VEHICLES AND THEIR USE

1. *Measures against air pollution by* **A1.62** *gases from positive-ignition engines of motor vehicles*:

Approximation of laws: Directive No 70/220/EEC of 20 March 1970 (JO 1970 L76) at p 1.

2. *Liquid fuel tanks and rear protective devices for motor vehicles and their trailers*:

Approximation of laws: Directive No 70/211/EEC of 20 March 1970 (JO 1970 L76) at p 23.

3. *Steering equipment for motor vehicles and their trailers*:

Approximation of laws: Directive No 70/311/EEC of 8 June 1970 (JO 1970 L133) at p 10.

4. *Type-approval of motor vehicles and their trailers*:

Approximation of laws: Directive No 70/156/EEC of 6 February 1970 (JO 1970 L42) at p 1.

5. *Permissible sound level and exhaust system of motor vehicles*:

Approximation of laws: Directive No 70/157/EEC of 6 February 1970 (JO 1970 L42) at p 16.

6. *Braking devices for certain categories of motor vehicles and their trailers*:

**A1.63** Approximation of laws: Directive No 71/320/EEC of 26 July 1971 (JO 1971 L202) at p 37.

7. *Insurance against civil liability in respect of the use of motor vehicles and the enforcement of the obligation to insure against such liability*:

Directive No 72/166/EEC of 24 April 1972 (JO 1972 L103) at p 1.

8. *Audible warning devices for motor vehicles*:

Directive No 70/388/EEC of 27 July 1970 (JO 1970 L176) at p 12.

9. *Doors of motor vehicles*:

Directive No 70/387/EEC of 27 July 1970 (JO 1970 L176) at p 5.

10. *Rear-view mirrors of motor vehicles*:

Directive No 71/127/EEC of 1 March 1971 (JO 1971 L68) at p 1.

11. *Measures against the emission of pollutants from diesel engines*:

Directive No 72/306/EEC of 2 August 1972 (JO 1972 L190) at p 1.

12. *Interior fittings of motor vehicles*:

Directive No 74/60/EEC of 17 December 1973 (OJ 1974 L38) at p 2.

13. *Devices to prevent the unauthorised use of motor vehicles*:

Directive No 74/61/EEC of 17 December 1973 (OJ 1974 L38) at p 22.


MATERIAL MEASURES OF LENGTH

Approximation of laws: Directive No **A1.64** 73/362/EEC of 19 November 1973 (OJ 1973 L335) at p 56.


ENLARGEMENT OF THE COMMUNITY

Amendment of certain Directives following the enlargement of the Community (OJ 1973 L326) at p 17.

# Appendix 2

# Council Resolution

of 19 May 1981
on a second programme of the European Economic Community
for a consumer protection and information policy

**A2.1**  THE COUNCIL OF THE EUROPEAN COMMUNITIES,

Having regard to the Treaty establishing the European Economic Community,

Having regard to the proposal from the Commission[1],

Having regard to the opinion of the European Parliament[2],

Having regard to the opinion of the Economic and Social Committee[3],

Whereas, pursuant to Article 2 of the Treaty, the task of the European Economic Community is to promote throughout the Community a harmonious development of economic activities, a continuous and balanced expansion and an accelerated raising of the standard of living;

Whereas the improvement of the quality of life is one of the tasks of the Community and as such implies protecting the health, safety and economic interests of the consumer;

Whereas fulfilment of this task requires a consumer protection and information policy to be implemented at Community level;

Whereas the Heads of State or of Government, meeting in Paris on 19 and 20 October 1972, confirmed this requirement by calling upon the institutions of the Communities to strengthen and co-ordinate measures for consumer protection;

Whereas the Council Resolution of 14 April 1975 provides for the implementation of a preliminary programme of the European Economic Community for a consumer protection and information policy[4];

Whereas the aims and principles of this policy have already been approved by the Council;

Whereas the preliminary programme of 14 April 1975 should be brought up to date to ensure the continuity of the measures already undertaken and enable new tasks to be undertaken in the years 1981 to 1986;

*Approves* the guidelines set out in the annexed action programme;  **A2.2**

*Notes* that the Commission will submit suitable proposals for the effective implementation of the programme;  **A2.3**

---

[1] OJ 1979 C218/3.
[2] OJ 1980 C291/35.
[3] OJ 1980 C83/24.
[4] OJ 1975 C92/1.

**A2.4**  *Undertakes* to act on these proposals, if possible within nine months of the date on which they are forwarded by the Commission or, if the case arises, of the date on which the opinions of the European Parliament and the Economic and Social Committee are forwarded.

---

## Annex

## Second programme of the European Economic Community for a consumer protection and information policy

I.  INTRODUCTION

**A2.5**  1.  The adoption by the Council on 14 April 1975 of a preliminary four-year programme of the European Economic Community for a consumer protection and information policy was the first stage in the Community's measures on behalf of consumers.

Measures taken or scheduled in accordance with the preliminary programme contribute towards improving the consumer's situation by protecting his health, his safety and his economic interest, by providing him with appropriate information and education, and by giving him a voice in decisions which involve him.

Very often these measures have also resulted in either eliminating non-tariff barriers to trade or harmonising the rules of competition by which manufacturers and retailers must abide.

**A2.6**  2.  The purpose of this programme is to enable the Community to continue and intensify its measures in this field and to help establish conditions for improved consultation between consumers on the one hand and manufacturers and retailers on the other.

This programme, for which it is appropriate to envisage a duration of five years if it is to be fully implemented, retains in its entirety the inspiration, objectives and underlying principles of the first. Like its predecessor, it is primarily concerned with the need to enable the consumer to act with full knowledge of the facts, and to hold the balance between market forces. To do this, he must be able to exercise the five basic rights which the preliminary programme conferred on him. They are:

– the right to protection of health and safety;
– the right to protection of economic interests;
– the right of redress;
– the right to information and education; and
– the right of representation (the right to be heard).

3.  Nevertheless in the current  **A2.7** difficult economic situation, a situation characterised by a slowdown in incomes growth, continuing unemployment, and the various economic consequences of the energy dependence which affects most Member States, consumers are obliged to pay more attention to the way in which they use their income, particularly as regards the quality of goods and services bought, so as to derive the maximum benefit from it. Very

special importance therefore attaches in this context to action relating to consumer protection with regard to the quality of goods and services, the conditions affecting their supply, and the provision of information about them. It follows, moreover, that, where appropriate, more attention than previously must be given to two questions which have assumed considerable importance for the consumer in the current economic climate, namely:

– the price of goods and services, regarding which the Community already exerts some influence, notably in the common agricultural policy but also in the competition policy,
– the quality of services (both public and private) which account for an ever-growing share of household expenditure.

**A2.8**  4. Moreover, without in any way ceasing to ensure that the rights listed above are complied with, the consumer policy, which has hitherto been mainly defensive, should become more positive and more open to a dialogue in order to establish the conditions in which the consumer can become a participant in the preparation and implementation of important economic decisions which concern him first and foremost as a buyer or a user, and which very largely determine his individual or collective living conditions. This approach corresponds to the spirit and the letter of the definition of the consumer given in the preliminary programme.[5] There are, however, several prerequisites to such a policy, notably:

(1) that while continuing to voice its proper concerns, the consumer movement will progressively take into account the economic and social implications of the decisions on which it might wish to be consulted;
(2) political and economic decision-makers should be willing to take consumers' views into account through the appropriate channels when preparing and implementing decisions which are likely to affect consumers' interests in the short or long term.

5. The Community's efforts should **A2.9** be directed towards fulfilling these prerequisites. Steps have already been taken along these lines. At Community level, consumer opinion has been taken more and more into consideration by Community bodies and institutions. For their part, consumer organisations are being progressively drawn into considering consumer policy in a wider context. Nevertheless, there is still some way to go. In particular the Community should try to encourage a dialogue and consultation between representatives from consumers and representatives from producers, distributors and suppliers of public or private services with a view, in certain cases, to arriving at solutions satisfactory to all the parties in question.

6. Although legislation both at **A2.10** national and Community level will still be needed in many cases in order to ensure that the consumer may exercise the fundamental rights listed above and that the market operates properly, the application of certain

---

[5] "The consumer is no longer seen merely as a purchaser and user of goods and services for personal, family or group purposes but also as a person concerned with the various facets of society which may affect him either directly or indirectly as a consumer."

principles might also be sought by other means, such as the establishment of specific agreements between the various interests held, which would have the advantage of giving consumers additional assurances of good trading practice.

The Commission will endeavour to facilitate the elaboration and conclusion of such agreements, on an experimental basis, for example, in certain fields of after-sales service and in areas involving aspects of professional ethics.

**A2.11** 7. Obviously, the use of this voluntary formula should in no case prejudice the application of existing laws and regulations, nor exclude the adoption of statutory and administrative provisions at either national or Community level.

**A2.12** 8. To sum up, the new programme is meant to:

(1) continue measures to protect and inform consumers, begun under the preliminary programme, the reasons for which and whose objectives and principles can only be confirmed. As a general rule, the Commission endeavours to take account of consumers' interests when framing any policy having a bearing on consumers, notably in regard to agriculture, competition and industrial policy. In such measures, besides questions of safety and quality, the problems posed by prices and their disparities and by the quality and prices of services cannot be ignored. With regard to prices, the Commission should give increasing attention to consumer interests in the definition and in the application of

Community policies (agricultural, competition, industrial, etc) which can influence those interests. It will also be appropriate to ensure that scientific enquiries into price disparities are pursued and made use of to a greater extent than in the past;

(2) seek to create the conditions for a better dialogue and closer consultation between representatives of consumers, producers and distributors.

## II. IMPLEMENTATION OF THE PROGRAMME

**A2.13** 9. The measures proposed in this programme are set out in the order of the objectives aimed at (already stated and approved in the preliminary programme), namely:

A. protection of consumers against health and safety hazards;

B. protection of consumers' economic interests;

C. improvement of the consumer's legal position (help, advice, the right to seek legal remedy);

D. improvement of consumer education and information;

E. appropriate consultation with and representation of consumers in the framing of decisions affecting their interests.

**A2.14** 10. The programme will be carried out, as was the preliminary one, by using the appropriate means laid down in the Treaty. Bearing in mind the number of interests involved, the Commission will undertake very wide consultations, notably through its Consultative Committees, before forwarding proposals for implementing measures.

**A2.15** 11. In addition, the Commission will

not fail to continue its close co-operation with international bodies such as the Council of Europe and the OECD which are concerned with consumer problems and to make use of their contributions in this field.

*A. Protection of consumer against health and safety hazards*

12. *Principles*

**A2.16** The preliminary programme laid down the following principles, which remain applicable:

(1) goods and services offered to consumers must be such that, under normal or foreseeable conditions of use, they present no risk to the health or safety of consumers. There should be quick and simple procedures for withdrawing them from the market in the event of their presenting such risks; in general, consumers should be informed in an appropriate manner of any risk liable to result from a foreseeable use of goods and services, taking account of the nature of the goods and services and of the persons for whom they are intended;

(2) the consumer must be protected against physical injury caused by defective products and services supplied by manufactures of goods and providers of services;

(3) substances or preparations which may be contained in or be added to foodstuffs should be defined and their use regulated, for example by endeavouring to draw up in Community rules, clear and precise positive lists. Any

processing which foodstuffs may undergo should also be defined and their use regulated where this is required to protect the consumer;

foodstuffs should not be adulterated or contaminated by packaging or other materials with which they come into contact, by their environment, by the conditions in which they are transported or stored or by persons coming into contact with them, in such a way that they affect the health or safety of consumers or otherwise become unfit for consumption;

(4) machines, appliances and electrical and electronic equipment and any other category of goods which may prejudicially affect the health and safety of consumers either in themselves or by their use, should be covered by special rules and be subject to a procedure recognised or approved by the public authorities (such as type approval or declaration of conformity with harmonised standards or rules) to ensure that they are safe for use;

(5) certain categories of new products which may prejudicially affect the health or safety of consumers should be made subject to special authorisation procedures harmonised throughout the Community.

13. *Priority measures*

On the basis of the principles set out **A2.17** above, the Commission will continue to expand its activities in accordance with the guidelines set out below, its prime objective being to make consumer goods and services safer to use and to promote consumer health protection. In addition, for goods or services which appear on the market or are developed in such a way as to jeopardise the safety or health of consumers, the Commission reserves the right to propose, if need be, suitable measures to supplement, pursuant to these principles, the priority measures already planned.

14.1 *Harmonisation of laws on certain products*

**A2.18** The Community will develop and pursue its work on harmonising the laws on certain products in order both to encourage the free movement of such goods and to regulate the marketing and use of substances or products likely to affect the health or safety of consumers. Harmonising measures will cover, as required, the properties of products, notification or approval procedures, methods of analysis and testing, labelling and safety standards. Moreover, an important part of these permanent activities is related to the application of Directives already in force or to be adopted as the programme is implemented, particularly in the framework of the committees on adaptation to technical progress.

All this work will be carried out with the help of the most reliable and advanced scientific and technical expertise available. The Commission will thus continue to consult the Scientific Committees for Animal Nutrition, Food, Pesticides, Cosmetology, Toxicology and Ecotoxicology.

Harmonisation will be directed chiefly towards the following types of product.

15.1 (a) *Foodstuffs*

**A2.19** The Community has developed two types of action with regard to foodstuffs, namely horizontal (general measures on additives, materials and objects coming into contact with foodstuffs, special foods) and vertical (measures on specific products).

The Commission will continue its work in this field by:

– monitoring the application of Council Directive 79/112/EEC of 18 December 1978 on the approximation of the laws of the Member States relating to the labelling, presentation and advertising of foodstuffs for sale to the ultimate consumer[6], particularly as regards misleading claims, the ingredients of alcoholic beverages, derogations regarding ingredients and the date of minimum durability of products;
– monitoring the adaptation of the Directives adopted to scientific and technical progress;
– introducing other measures on, for example, flavouring, surface sprays used on fruit, vegetables and cheeses, baby foods, deep-frozen foods and pesticide residues;
– putting forward suitable proposals when consumer health problems arise unexpectedly (as has already occurred with erucic acid, vinyl chloride monomer residues and saccharine);
– examining certain nutrition problems (effects of certain foodstuffs on health, food labelling, etc), in particular as regards consumer education and information; if necessary, it will submit appropriate proposals;
– participating in standardisation activities in the Codex alimentarius, with particular reference to

---

[6] OJ 1979 L33 at p 1.

the implementation or preparation of guidelines.

16.1 (b)  *Cosmetics*

**A2.20**  Council Directive 76/768/EEC of 27 July 1976 on the approximation of the laws of the Member States relating to cosmetic products[7] enumerates a number of tasks of a scientific and technical nature which will be performed; these include:

– permitting or prohibiting the substances listed in Annex IV to the Directive which are at present provisionally allowed;

– drawing up, on the basis of scientific and technical research, proposals for lists of authorised substances which could include antioxidants, hair dyes, preservatives and ultraviolet filters, taking into account in particular the problem of sensitisation;

– adapting the Directive to technical progress, particularly by introducing the methods of analysis necessary for checking the composition of cosmetic products, by determining criteria of microbiological and chemical purity and methods for checking compliance with these criteria and finally, possibly by amending Annex II to the Directive, which lists substances which cosmetic products must not contain.

17.1 (c)  *Textiles*

**A2.21**  With regard to the safety of textiles, the Commission will continue to study problems of textile inflammability, with particular reference to health risks liable to result from the use of fire-proofing substances.

The Commission will likewise examine risks arising from the use of raw materials or other substances such as colouring agents.

18.1 (d)  *Toys*

The work already in hand as part of **A2.22** the proposal for a Directive on the approximation of the laws of the Member States concerning toy safety[8] will be continued and proposals for directives will be prepared on the physical and mechanical safety, inflammability, toxicity and electrical safety of toys.

19.1 (e)  *Pharmaceutical products*

Several Directives have been adopted **A2.23** on pharmaceutical products for human use, particularly on conditions of marketing, provisions on standards and protocols and the colouring agents used. In addition, two proposals for directives are now being discussed on pharmaceutical products for veterinary use which may have indirect influence on consumer health. The Commission will continue its work in this area and in particular submit to the Council a proposal for a Directive on the advertising of pharmaceutical products.

20.1 (f)  *Dangerous substances*

The Commission will continue its **A2.24** work on dangerous substances for which there are already Directives on classification, labelling, packaging and use, and will concentrate on dangerous preparations. In particular, the Commission will study the safety problems associated with household use of products in which such preparations are employed (cleaning materials, for example) and, if necessary, submit appropriate proposals.

---

[7] OJ 1976 L262 at p 169.
[8] OJ 1980 C228 at p 10.

21.1 (g)  *Tobacco and alcohol*

**A2.25**  After carrying out comparative studies on measures taken or planned by Member States with regard to tobacco and alcohol, the Commission will:

    –  assess to what extent divergences in measures taken by Member States in regard to these products affect the Community market and, where necessary, make appropriate proposals;

    –  take such other initiatives, in support of actions undertaken in Member States, as may be appropriate in the more general context of problems associated with the use or abuse of such products by consumers.

22.1 (h)  *Manufactured products*

**A2.26**  The Commission will continue its work on motor vehicle components and other manufactured products likely to affect consumer safety and health.

In particular, the problem of the inflammability of materials used in manufacturing furniture or for fitting out buildings (furnishing materials in general and various internal and external covering materials) will be examined.

23.2  *Monitoring product safety*

**A2.27**  Implementation of measures adopted in various fields concerning the protection of consumer health and safety in respect of which action to harmonise laws has already been taken (food additives, cosmetics and pesticides) requires the national authorities supervising their application constantly to improve the methods used, in line with industrial developments and the advance of

scientific knowledge; there are largely similar problems in making such improvements in all the Member States, particularly when it comes to working out ways and means.

The Community should therefore draw up a list of control systems in Member States in order to remedy any difficulties or shortcomings, for example, by developing more effective control methods or by the exchange of experts or information between laboratories.

To this end, the Commission will organise meetings between representatives of specialised laboratories existing in the Member States and, if necessary, submit appropriate proposals to the Council.

24.3  *Research*

The commission will continue to **A2.28** examine the results of studies in the various fields likely to further the cause of product safety and, where appropriate, will take steps to co-ordinate and encourage such studies.

25.4  *Information on products*

To comply with the principles set out **A2.29** above, the fullest and most objective information possible must be available on the various aspects of product safety. This information should suggest the direction the work should take by facilitating the selection of priorities.

26.(a)  With this in view, the **A2.30** Commission has already sent the Council a proposal for a Decision introducing a Community system of information on accidents in which products are involved, outside the spheres of occupational activities and road traffic[9]; the purpose of this

---

[9] OJ 1978 C252 at p 2.

system would be to enable detailed statistics to be compiled.

(b) In addition, with a view to promoting objective and detailed documentation on the properties of products likely to affect consumer health and safety, the Commission will, by taking appropriate steps, endeavour to survey existing data bank systems, further their development and facilitate access to them.

**A2.31** 27. As the information system referred to in point 26 is not designed for adopting emergency measures, the Commission has proposed that a system be set up at Community level for the rapid exchange of information on dangers arising from the use of consumer goods. Such a system would enable the responsible authorities to take necessary measures promptly to ensure public safety.

*B.   Protection of the economic interests of consumers*

28. *Principles*

**A2.32** The preliminary programme set out a number of principles which are still relevant:

(1) purchasers of goods or services should be protected against certain unfair sales practices and in particular against the vendor's standard contracts, the exclusion of essential rights in contracts, harsh conditions of credit, demands for payment for unsolicited goods and high-pressure selling methods;

(2) the consumer should be protected against damage to

his economic interests caused by defective products or unsatisfactory services;

(3) the presentation and promotion of goods and services, including financial services, should not be designed to mislead, either directly or indirectly, the person to whom they are offered or by whom they have been requested;

(4) no form of advertising should mislead the potential buyer of the product or service. An advertiser in any medium must be able to justify, by appropriate means, the validity of any claims he makes[10];

(5) all information provided on labels at the point of sale or in advertisements must be accurate;

(6) the consumer is entitled to reliable after-sales service for consumer durables, including the provision of spare parts required to carry out repairs;

(7) the range of goods available to consumers should be such that as far as possible consumers are offered an adequate choice.

29. On the basis of these principles **A2.33** and pursuant to the preliminary programme, the Commission has submitted proposals for Directives which are still under discussion by the Council bodies.

The following are the texts concerned:

– a proposal for a Directive to protect the consumer in respect of contracts which have been negotiated away from business premises[11];

---

[10] This principle will apply in observance of existing criminal law provisions in the Member States.
[11] OJ 1977 C22 at p 6.

- a proposal for a Directive relating to the approximation of the laws, regulations and administrative provisions of the Member States concerning misleading and unfair advertising[12];
- a proposal for a Directive relating to the approximation of the laws, regulations and administrative provisions of Member States concerning liability for defective products[13];
- a proposal for a Directive relating to the approximation of the laws, regulations and administrative provisions of the Member States concerning consumer credit[14].

30. *Continuation of action provided for under the preliminary programme*

**A2.34**  The Commission will pursue the action already begun under the 1975 programme which it has not been able to bring to a conclusion, particularly as regards certain unfair commercial practices.

The Commission has already started work on unfair terms in contracts, with the help of government experts, as a basis for a Community measure. Meanwhile, legislation has been adopted in several Member States, and the Commission will submit, as a first step, a discussion paper in which it will set out all the problems which this subject involves and the various options open with a view to harmonising those aspects of competition which may be affected by disparities in this area. After wide-ranging consultations on this discussion paper, the Commission will put forward suitable proposals, where necessary.

31.  Within the framework of the **A2.35** general activities already undertaken, the Commission will also study the promotion of the interests of specific groups of underprivileged consumers in order to cater better for their particular needs.

Action taken by the Commission on competition, pursuant to Articles 85 and 86 of the Treaty, contributes to this end in being opposed to certain business practices likely to have a detrimental effect on consumer prices or in being intended to prevent such practices.

32.  Under the common agricultural **A2.36** policy, the Commission has taken into consideration the effects of the common farm prices and the level of supplies on the Community market on the interests of consumers, as envisaged among the objectives of Article 39 of the Treaty. The Commission has also consulted consumers when drawing up the price proposals submitted to the Council.

The Commission will continue to take consumer interests into account in the implementation of this policy.

33.  In general, it is important to take **A2.37** into consideration the economic repercussions which certain factors such as the scarcity of resources, shorter working hours and the use of new data-processing and telecommunications technology may have on consumption patterns and producer–distributor–consumer relations. The Commission will carry out further

---

[12] OJ 1978 C70 at p 4.
[13] OJ 1976 C241 at p 9.
[14] OJ 1979 C80 at p 4.

studies and will submit suitable proposals, where necessary.

34. *Expansion of Community action on services*

**A2.38** Because of the growth in the number and importance of services, the part they take up in household expenditure and the opening of the frontiers of Member States to an increasing number of them, there should be a strengthening of consumer protection in this sector, notably in the matter of quality of services and their price transparency.[15]

Services account for a growing proportion of economic activity in the Member States of the Community, where they employ on average about half the working population and are a field in which manpower often represents a high proportion of added value. The term "services" in fact covers a very wide range of activities, in which changes in productivity vary considerably from one to another. However, it is possible to identify three broadly common features:

- expenditure on services is increasing rapidly in absolute terms and as a proportion of the household budget;
- whereas the quality and performance of industrial products can be defined with a relatively high degree of objectivity, any assessment of the quality of a service rendered is often more subjective and thus the comparison becomes less reliable;
- a large (sometimes the largest) proportion of service activities consists of collective services where the public sector or the

quasi-public sector has a near monopoly on supply and where market forces operate only partially, as regards both the fixing of prices and determination of the quality of the service offered.

The Commission will study the following three areas and, if appropriate, put forward suitable proposals. With due regard for the significance of such measures for consumer protection and the effects of differences in Member States' legislation on the proper functioning of the Common Market.

35.(a) *Commercial services connected with products*

The terms of after-sales service for **A2.39** consumer durables are of particular importance, especially in view of the increased useful life of certain goods. With this in mind, the Commission will examine ways of improving the quality of the after-sales service provided by producers and suppliers and by undertakings which carry out maintenance and repairs, in particular as regards the guarantee period, wider use of firm estimates, the drawing up of detailed invoices, product transport and out-of-service costs, and the availability of replacement parts.

The Commission will study the means necessary for this purpose and will take the appropriate steps with a view to improving conditions of warranty on the part of the producer and/or supplier and after-sales service either by legislation or, where appropriate, by agreements between the parties concerned for *inter alia* the improvement of

---

[15] In view of the increasing importance of this sector, the Commission organised a colloquium of consumer organisations on the theme "The consumer as user of services" in October 1979.

contract terms. Priority will be given to warranties and services associated with motor vehicles and electrical household appliances.

36.(b) *Commercial services not connected with products*

**A2.40**  This heading covers a wide variety of activities of increasing importance in meeting the needs of consumers, both as individuals and collectively, particularly tourism, consumer credit and insurance. The Commission will carry out studies on the development of these services and how they are provided. If necessary, the Commission will put suitable proposals to the Council and/or encourage the adoption of voluntary agreements for improving the general conditions under which these services are provided.

37.(c) *Public and quasi-public services*

**A2.41**  A number of services essential to consumers are provided by public and quasi-public services, notably electricity, gas and water supplies and transport. In these areas consultation should be encouraged between the main public services and administrative authorities of a commercial character and the representatives of consumers. To this end, the Commission will prepare a report on consumer representation, concentrating on those services which are international in character, with a view to putting forward suitable proposals, where necessary.

C.  *Advice, help and redress*

38.  *Principles*

**A2.42**  The preliminary programme states that "consumers should receive advice and help in respect of complaints and of injury or damage resulting from purchase or use of defective goods or unsatisfactory services" and that "consumers are also entitled to proper redress for such injury or damage by means of swift, effective and inexpensive procedures".

In 1975 the Commission held a symposium on legal and extra-legal means of consumer protection which in particular made it possible to analyse:

– systems of assistance and advice in the Member States;
– systems of redress, arbitration and the amicable settlement of disputes in the Member States;
– the laws of the Member States relating to consumer protection in the courts, particularly the various means of, and procedures for, obtaining legal remedy, including actions brought by consumer associations or other bodies;
– systems and laws of the kind referred to above in certain third countries.

Suggestions put forward at the symposium can be classified under five heads:

1. the need to improve consumer information and education;
2. the need to set up conciliation bodies either to take preventive action to put an end to certain reprehensible practices by amicable arrangement, or to settle by mutual agreement disputes between consumers and tradesmen or suppliers of services;
3. the setting up of arbitration bodies;
4. the simplification of legal procedures for settling disputes over small sums of money;

5. assigning responsibility for consumer protection to consumer groups, public authorities or institutions like the ombudsman.

This matter has already been the subject of a most constructive debate in the European Parliament and the Economic and Social Committee.

Although limited, the Community's action in this area will seek to make a useful contribution to the implementation of suggestions made in the analysis referred to above. The work done by the Council of Europe on legal aid will also be drawn upon, as well as the studies undertaken by the European University Institute in Florence.

39. *Priority measures*

**A2.43** The Commission will continue to study the procedures and channels for obtaining legal remedy which exist in the Member States, particularly with regard to the right of consumer associations to institute legal proceedings, the simplification of court procedures and the processing of individual petitions, the development of amicable settlement procedures and the admissibility of proceedings by consumers against public undertakings administered according to commercial criteria. It will publish a discussion paper on all these matters, taking into account the different experience gained and the procedures applied in the Member States.

The Commission will also continue, where necessary, to encourage national or local schemes facilitating consumers' access to the courts and the settlement of the more common or minor disputes, and will publish the results.

D. *Consumer information and education*

40. *Consumer information*

**Principles**

Sufficient information should be **A2.44** available to the purchaser of goods or services, and to the general public, to enable him to:

– assess the basic features of the goods and services offered, such as the nature, quality, quantity, energy consumption and price;
– make a rational choice between competing products and services;
– use these products and services safely and to his satisfaction;
– claim redress for any injury or damage resulting from the product supplied or service received.

Following a study of the feasibility and value of drawing up general rules on labelling for all mass-consumption non-food products, it would appear to be more useful to work out rules for each specific category of products so that they are more directly related to the properties of each product.

41. *Priority measures*

Under this programme, the Commis- **A2.45** sion will take the following measures:

– include in any proposals on given products or services which it puts to the Council special provisions to take account of their specific properties, with the aim of guaranteeing that the consumer receives proper information on the properties and the quality of the goods and services supplied;
– organise consultation meetings between the representatives of consumers, producers, distributors and suppliers of services as a

means of promoting the introduction and development of a voluntary labelling system or of any other voluntary means (such as instructions for use or packaging) of informing consumers about the capabilities of certain kinds of products or services;

— encourage co-operation between bodies carrying out comparative testing, particularly in the case of tests on products and services which are available in several Member States at the same time;

— conduct a more general information campaign on national and Community activities which are directly or indirectly relevant to the interests of consumers by[16]:

— regularly publishing press releases and by holding briefing sessions for radio and television reporters and for the specialised press of consumer associations;

— organising meetings of consumer organisations to enable them to discuss the development of the consumer movement in Europe and of consumer protection in the Community;

— publishing a periodical report on the state of consumer protection in the Community which will cover the work done in this field and the development of the consumer movement at Community and national level.

**A2.46**  42. In implementing this programme, particular attention will be paid to information on prices. This is essential for the proper functioning of competition, which can also be expected to have a positive effect in attenuating inflationary forces, and for ensuring a better choice for consumers.

It is important that as far as possible the market itself should be so structured as to facilitate the adjustment of demand to price changes, primarily through increased transparency. This implies in appropriate cases action in three directions:

— the consumer should be informed about the value for money of products and services (particularly as regards conditions of warranty and after-sales service) on offer by means of fuller information on products, wider publication of the results of comparative tests and the provision of information to consumers on identical products which they cannot recognise as such;

— the consumer should be informed about prices themselves by improvement of the regulations on price marking, including prices per unit of measurement, although no encouragement must be given to price-fixing practices that may adversely affect competition;

— the consumer should be informed about price differences, particularly in the localities accessible to him, by the encouragement of local or regional schemes for this purpose.

43. To this end the Commission will **A2.47** take supplementary measures which must in no case be price-control or

---

[16] As part of its general information policy, the Commission will endeavour to take specific steps to inform the general public of the present Community programme, the activities undertaken and the results obtained.

price-fixing measures but must supply appropriate information to several different sections of the public. The Commission will endeavour to promote private initiatives aimed at improving consumer information on prices and comparative prices at local or regional level.

As regards price formation, the Commission will also continue to exercise its powers with regard to rules of competition under Articles 85 and 86 of the Treaty.

CONSUMER EDUCATION

44. *Principle*

**A2.48** In this area of policy, the preliminary programme states:

"Facilities should be made available to children as well as to young people and adults to educate them to act as discriminating consumers, capable of making an informed choice of goods and services and conscious of their rights and responsibilities. To this end, consumers should, in particular, benefit from basic information on the principle of modern economics."

45 *Priority measures*

**A2.49** 1.  Given the powers of the Member States with regard to education and the work the Commission has already undertaken, Community action will consist in continuing the wide-ranging exchange of views on national experience and joint con-

sideration of the aims and methods of consumer education in schools.

With this in mind, the Commission will submit to the Council a communication on consumer training.

2.  It will look into possibilities in adult education, and in particular into possibilities for televised courses and study leave for officials and members of consumer associations.

3.  It will give consideration to the problems which arise for under-privileged consumers.

*E.  Promotion of consumer interests*

46. The preliminary programme **A2.50** gave priority to measures to protect consumer interests. In the course of its implementation, the idea gradually developed that the consumer should be increasingly seen as having a part to play in the preparation of economic and social decisions concerning him.

47.  This development is based on a **A2.51** number of considerations.

The first is the value of a dialogue between consumers and producers/distributors and between consumers and the public authorities. This becomes clear once we recognise that in our society changes in economic and social policy must as far as possible be the result of consultation between all the parties concerned, including consumers, and that consumption should no longer be regarded merely as a balancing variable of economic development.

The second consideration is the development of closer co-operation between associations which could defend and promote consumers' interests and play an active part in trying to achieve the necessary balance between consumers and producers/distributors. It must be recognised that action by the individual consumer is not likely to have much effect on the mass market where he exercises his choice, while excessive growth in regulatory powers can only serve to over-institutionalise the relationships between the parties concerned.

**A2.52** 48. Promotion of the consumer's interests could be based on the following:

– development of procedures for consultation by the public authorities, to the appropriate extent, of representatives of consumer interests;

– development of a regular dialogue between representatives of consumer interests and producers' and distributors' organisations;

– more aid to organisations which represent consumers.

49. *Priority measures*

**A2.53** Under this programme, the Commission will:

– send the Council a communica-

tion on consumer association representation, criteria for representation and the approval procedures operating in Member States. At the same time it will give details of the extent of consumer representation within the Community;

– continue to ensure that there is balanced representation of consumers on the specialised advisory committees set up by the Commission;

– continue, and where possible increase, its aid to European consumer associations to enable them to make their viewpoint better heard, and it will also make every effort to organise seminars for training officials from these associations, particularly on the subject of common policies;

– foster consultation between European consumer associations and the various business interests concerned on specific matters of common interest;

– endeavour to promote adequate representation of consumers in standards organisations.

# Appendix 3

# Council Directive 93/13/EEC

of 5 April 1993 on Unfair Terms in Consumer Contracts
(OJ 1993 L95/29)

**A3.1**  THE COUNCIL OF THE EUROPEAN COMMUNITIES,

Having regard to the Treaty establishing the European Economic Community, and in particular Article 100A thereof,

Having regard to the proposal from the Commission (OJ 1992 C73/7),

In co-operation with the European Parliament (OJ 1991 C326/108; OJ 1993 C21/1),

Having regard to the opinion of the Economic and Social Committee (OJ 1991 C159/34),

**A3.2**  Whereas it is necessary to adopt measures with the aim of progressively establishing the internal market before 31 December 1992; whereas the internal market comprises an area without internal frontiers in which goods, persons, services and capital move freely;

Whereas the laws of Member States relating to the terms of contract between the seller of goods or supplier of services, on the one hand, and the consumer of them, on the other hand, show many disparities, with the result that the national markets for the sale of goods and services to consumers differ from each other and that distortions of competition may arise amongst the sellers and suppliers, notably when they sell and supply in other Member States;

**A3.3**  Whereas, in particular, the laws of Member States relating to unfair terms in consumer contracts show marked divergences;

Whereas it is the responsibility of the Member States to ensure that contracts concluded with consumers do not contain unfair terms;

Whereas, generally speaking, consumers do not know the rules of law which, in Member States other than their own, govern contracts for the sale of goods or services; whereas this lack of awareness may deter them from direct transactions for the purchase of goods or services in another Member State;

**A3.4**  Whereas, in order to facilitate the establishment of the internal market and to safeguard the citizen in his role as consumer when acquiring goods and services under contracts which are governed by the laws of Member States other than his own, it is essential to remove unfair terms from those contracts;

Whereas sellers of goods and suppliers of services will thereby be helped in their task of selling goods and supplying services, both at home and throughout the internal market; whereas competition will thus be stimulated, so contributing to increased choice for Community citizens as consumers;

**A3.5** Whereas the two Community programmes for a consumer protection and information policy (OJ 1975 C92/1; OJ 1981 C133/1) underlined the importance of safeguarding consumers in the matter of unfair terms of contract; whereas this protection ought to be provided by laws and regulations which are either harmonised at Community level or adopted directly at that level;

Whereas in accordance with the principle laid down under the heading "Protection of the economic interests of the consumers", as stated in those programmes: "acquirers of goods and services should be protected against the abuse of power by the seller or supplier, in particular against one-sided standard contracts and the unfair exclusion of essential rights in contracts";

**A3.6** Whereas more effective protection of the consumer can be achieved by adopting uniform rules of law in the matter of unfair terms; whereas those rules should apply to all contracts concluded between sellers or suppliers and consumers; whereas as a result *inter alia* contracts relating to employment, contracts relating to succession rights, contracts relating to rights under family law and contracts relating to the incorporation and organisation of companies or partnership agreements must be excluded from this Directive;

Whereas the consumer must receive equal protection under contracts concluded by word of mouth and written contracts regardless, in the latter case, of whether the terms of the contract are contained in one or more documents;

**A3.7** Whereas, however, as they now stand, national laws allow only partial harmonisation to be envisaged; whereas, in particular, only contractual terms which have not been individually negotiated are covered by this Directive; whereas Member States should have the option, with due regard for the Treaty, to afford consumers a higher level of protection through national provisions that are more stringent than those of this Directive;

Whereas the statutory or regulatory provisions of the Member States which directly or indirectly determine the terms of consumer contracts are presumed not to contain unfair terms; whereas, therefore, it does not appear to be necessary to subject the terms which reflect mandatory statutory or regulatory provisions and the principles or provisions of international conventions to which the Member States or the Community are party; whereas in that respect the wording "mandatory statutory or regulatory provisions" in Article 1(2) also covers rules which, according to the law, shall apply between the contracting parties provided that no other arrangements have been established;

**A3.8** Whereas Member States must however ensure that unfair terms are not included, particularly because this Directive also applies to trades, business or professions of a public nature;

Whereas it is necessary to fix in a general way the criteria for assessing the unfair character of contract terms;

Whereas the assessment, according to the general criteria chosen, of the unfair character of terms, in particular in sale or supply activities of a public nature providing collective services which take account of solidarity among users, must be supplemented by a means of making an overall evaluation of the different interests involved; whereas this constitutes the requirement of good faith; whereas, in making an assessment of good faith, particular regard shall be had to the strength of the bargaining positions of the parties, whether the consumer had an inducement to agree to the term and whether the goods or services were sold or supplied to the special order of the consumer; whereas the requirement of good faith may be satisfied by the seller or supplier where he deals fairly and equitably with the other party whose legitimate interests he has to take into account;

**A3.9**  Whereas, for the purposes of this Directive, the annexed list of terms can be of indicative value only and, because of the cause of the minimal character of the Directive, the scope of these terms may be the subject of amplification or more restrictive editing by the Member States in their national laws;

Whereas the nature of goods or services should have an influence on assessing the unfairness of contractual terms;

**A3.10**  Whereas, for the purposes of this Directive, assessment of unfair character shall not be made of terms which describe the main subject matter of the contract nor the quality/price ratio of the goods or services supplied; whereas the main subject matter of the contract and the price/quality ratio may nevertheless be taken into account in assessing the fairness of other terms; whereas it follows, *inter alia*, that in insurance contracts, the terms which clearly define or circumscribe the insured risk and the insurer's liability shall not

be subject to such assessment since these restrictions are taken into account in calculating the premium paid by the consumer;

Whereas contracts should be drafted in plain, intelligible language, the consumer should actually be given an opportunity to examine all the terms and, if in doubt, the interpretation most favourable to the consumer should prevail;

**A3.11**  Whereas Member States should ensure that unfair terms are not used in contracts concluded with consumers by a seller or supplier and that if, nevertheless, such terms are so used, they will not bind the consumer, and the contract will continue to bind the parties upon those terms if it is capable of continuing in existence without the unfair provisions;

Whereas there is a risk that, in certain cases, the consumer may be deprived of protection under this Directive by designating the law of a non-Member country as the law applicable to the contract; whereas provisions should therefore be included in this Directive designed to avert this risk;

**A3.12**  Whereas persons or organisations, if regarded under the law of a Member State as having a legitimate interest in the matter, must have facilities for initiating proceedings concerning terms of contract drawn up for general use in contracts concluded with consumers, and in particular unfair terms, either before a court or before an administrative authority competent to decide upon complaints or to initiate appropriate legal proceedings; whereas this possibility does not, however, entail prior verification of the general conditions obtaining in individual economic sectors;

Whereas the courts or administrative authorities of the Member States must have at their disposal adequate and effective means of preventing the continued application of unfair terms in consumer contracts,

HAS ADOPTED THIS DIRECTIVE:

*Article 1*

**A3.13** 1. The purpose of this Directive is to approximate the laws, regulations and administrative provisions of the Member States relating to unfair terms in contracts concluded between a seller or supplier and a consumer.

2. The contractual terms which reflect mandatory statutory or regulatory provisions and the provisions or principles of international conventions to which the Member States or the Community are party, particularly in the transport area, shall not be subject to the provisions of this Directive.

*Article 2*

**A3.14** For the purposes of this Directive:

(a) "unfair terms" means the contractual terms defined in Article 3;

(b) "consumer" means any natural person who, in contracts covered by this Directive, is acting for purposes which are outside his trade, business or profession;

(c) "seller or supplier" means any natural or legal person who, in contracts covered by this Directive, is acting for purposes relating to his trade, business or profession, whether publicly owned or privately owned.

*Article 3*

1. A contractual term which has not **A3.15** been individually negotiated shall be regarded as unfair if, contrary to the requirement of good faith, it causes a significant imbalance in the parties' rights and obligations arising under the contract, to the detriment of the consumer.

2. A term shall always be regarded as not individually negotiated where it has been drafted in advance and the consumer has therefore not been able to influence the substance of the term, particularly in the context of a pre-formulated standard contract.

The fact that certain aspects of a term or one specific term have been individually negotiated shall not exclude the application of this Article to the rest of a contract if an overall assessment of the contract indicates that it is nevertheless a pre-formulated standard contract.

Where any seller or supplier claims **A3.16** that a standard term has been individually negotiated, the burden of proof in this respect shall be incumbent on him.

3. The Annex shall contain an indicative and non-exhaustive list of the terms which may be regarded as unfair.

*Article 4*

1. Without prejudice to Article 7, **A3.17** the unfairness of a contractual term shall be assessed, taking

into account the nature of the goods or services for which the contract was concluded and by referring, at the time of conclusion of the contract, to all the circumstances attending the conclusion of the contract and to all the other terms of the contract or of another contract on which it is dependent.

2. Assessment of the unfair nature of the terms shall relate neither to the definition of the main subject matter of the contract nor to the adequacy of the price and remuneration, on the one hand, as against the services or goods supplied in exchange, on the other, in so far as these terms are in plain intelligible language.

### Article 5

**A3.18** In the case of contracts where all or certain terms offered to the consumer are in writing, these terms must always be drafted in plain, intelligible language. Where there is doubt about the meaning of a term, the interpretation most favourable to the consumer shall prevail. This rule on interpretation shall not apply in the context of the procedures laid down in Article 7(2).

### Article 6

**A3.19** 1. Member States shall lay down the unfair terms used in a contract concluded with a consumer by a seller or supplier shall, as provided for under their national law, not be binding on the consumer and that the contract shall continue to bind the parties upon those terms if it is capable of continuing in existence without the unfair terms.

2. Member States shall take the necessary measures to ensure that the consumer does not lose the protection granted by this Directive by virtue of the choice of the law of a non-Member country as the law applicable to the contract if the latter has a close connection with the territory of the Member States.

### Article 7

**A3.20** 1. Member States shall ensure that, in the interests of consumers and of competitors, adequate and effective means exist to prevent the continued use of unfair terms in contracts concluded with consumers by sellers or suppliers.

2. The means referred to in paragraph 1 shall include provisions whereby persons or organisations, having a legitimate interest under national law in protecting consumers, may take action according to the national law concerned before the courts or before competent administrative bodies for a decision as to whether contractual terms drawn up for general use are unfair, so that they can apply appropriate and effective means to prevent the continued use of such terms.

**A3.21** 3. With due regard for national laws, the legal remedies referred to in paragraph 2 may be directed separately or jointly against a number of sellers or suppliers from the same economic sector or their associations which use or recommend the use of the same general contractual terms or similar terms.

*Article 8*

**A3.22** Member States may adopt or retain the most stringent provisions compatible with the Treaty in the area covered by this Directive, to ensure a maximum degree of protection for the consumer.

*Article 9*

**A3.23** The Commission shall present a report to the European Parliament and to the Council concerning the application of this Directive five years at the latest after the date in Article 10(1).

*Article 10*

**A3.24** 1. Member States shall bring into force the laws, regulations and administrative provisions necessary to comply with this Directive no later than 31 December 1994. They shall forthwith inform the Commission thereof. These provisions shall be applicable to all contracts concluded after 31 December 1994.

2. When Member States adopt these measures, they shall contain a reference to this Directive or shall be accompanied by such reference on the occasion of their official publication. The methods of making such a reference shall be laid down by the Member States.

3. Member States shall communicate the main provisions of national law which they adopt in the field covered by this Directive to the Commission.

*Article 11*

This Directive is addressed to the **A3.25** Member States.

Done at Luxembourg, 5 April 1993.

For the Council, The President N. HELVEG PETERSEN

---

**Annex**

Terms Referred to in Article 3(3)

**A3.26** **1. Terms which have the object or effect of:**

  (a) excluding or limiting the legal liability of a seller or supplier in the event of the death of a consumer or personal injury to the latter resulting from an act or omission of that seller or supplier;

  (b) inappropriately excluding or limiting the legal rights of the consumer *vis-à-vis* the seller or supplier or another party in the event of total or partial non-performance or inadequate performance by the seller or supplier of any of the contractual obligations, including the option of offsetting a debt owed to the seller or supplier against any claim which the consumer may have against him;

  (c) making an agreement binding on the consumer whereas

provision of services by the seller or supplier is subject to a condition whose realisation depends on his own will alone;

**A3.27** (d) permitting the seller or supplier to retain sums paid by the consumer where the latter decides not to conclude or perform the contract, without providing for the consumer to receive compensation of an equivalent amount from the seller or supplier where the latter is the party cancelling the contract;

(e) requiring any consumer who fails to fulfil his obligation to pay a disproportionately high sum in compensation;

(f) authorising the seller or supplier to dissolve the contract on a discretionary basis where the same facility is not granted to the consumer, or permitting the seller or supplier to retain the sums paid for services not yet supplied by him where it is the seller or supplier himself who dissolves the contract;

**A3.28** (g) enabling the seller or supplier to terminate a contract of indeterminate duration without reasonable notice except where there are serious grounds for doing so;

(h) automatically extending a contract of fixed duration where the consumer does not indicate otherwise, when the deadline fixed for the consumer to express this desire not to extend the contract is unreasonably early;

(i) irrevocably binding the consumer to terms with which he had no real opportunity of becoming acquainted before the conclusion of the contract;

(j) enabling the seller or supplier **A3.29** to alter the terms of the contract unilaterally without a valid reason which is specified in the contract;

(k) enabling the seller or supplier to alter unilaterally without a valid reason any characteristics of the product or service to be provided;

(l) providing for the price of goods to be determined at the time of delivery or allowing a seller of goods or supplier of services to increase their price without in both cases giving the consumer the corresponding right to cancel the contract if the final price is too high in relation to the price agreed when the contract was concluded;

(m) giving the seller or supplier the **A3.30** right to determine whether the goods or services supplied are in conformity with the contract, or giving him the exclusive right to interpret any term of the contract;

(n) limiting the seller's or supplier's obligation to respect commitments undertaken by his agents or making his commitments subject to compliance with a particular formality;

(o) obliging the consumer to fulfil all his obligations where the seller or supplier does not perform his;

(p) giving the seller or supplier the **A3.31** possibility of transferring his rights and obligations under the contract, where this may serve to reduce the guarantees for the consumer, without the latter's agreement;

(q) excluding or hindering the consumer's right to take legal action or exercise any other legal remedy, particularly by requiring the consumer to take disputes exclusively to arbitration not covered by legal provisions, unduly restricting the evidence available to him or imposing on him a burden of proof which, according to the applicable law, should lie with another party to the contract.

**2. Scope of subparagraphs (g), (j) and (l)**

**A3.32** (a) Subparagraph (g) is without hindrance to terms by which a supplier of financial services reserves the right to terminate unilaterally a contract of indeterminate duration without notice where there is a valid reason, provided that the supplier is required to inform the other contracting party or parties thereof immediately.

(b) Subparagraph (j) is without hindrance to terms under which a supplier of financial services reserves the right to alter the rate of interest payable by the consumer or due to the latter, or the amount of other charges for financial services without notice where there is a valid reason, provided that the supplier is required to inform the other contracting party or parties thereof at the earliest opportunity and that the latter are free to dissolve the contract immediately.

Subparagraph (j) is also without **A3.33** hindrance to terms under which a seller or supplier reserves the right to alter unilaterally the conditions of a contract of indeterminate duration, provided that he is required to inform the consumer with reasonable notice and that the consumer is free to dissolve the contract.

(c) Subparagraphs (g), (j) and (l) do not apply to:

- transactions in transferable securities, financial instruments and other products or services where the price is linked to fluctuations in a stock exchange quotation or index or a financial market rate that the seller or supplier does not control;

- contracts for the purchase or sale of foreign currency, traveller's cheques or international money orders denominated in foreign currency;

(d) Subparagraph (l) is without hindrance to price-indexation clauses, where lawful, provided that the method by which prices vary is explicitly described.

# Index

# Index